DAYBREAK
&
EVENTIDE

A Little Book of Prayers & Worship
for Individuals, Small Groups
& House Churches

Andrew J. Brown
John C. Morgan

Lighthouse Editions for the
The Unitarian Christian Association
CAMBRIDGE MMVII

Published by
LIGHTHOUSE EDITIONS
13 Brandon Court, Cambridge CB1 1DZ
for the
THE UNITARIAN CHRISTIAN ASSOCIATION
www.unitarianchristian.org.uk
5 Emmanuel Road, Cambridge CB1 1JW
ISBN 978-1-904998-03-7

Cover design by Mark Argent (www.markargent.com)
Typeset in ITC Stone
Printed by Trimprint Ltd, Armagh, N. Ireland (028) 3752 2063

"To Thee our morning song of praise,
To Thee our evening prayers we raise...."
Ambrose

"And in the morning, a great while before
day, he rose and went out to a lonely place,
and there he prayed."
Mark 1:35 (KJV)

"Thine is the day, thine also the night."
Psalm 74:16 (KJV)

"Preach the Universal and Everlasting Gospel of Boundless,
Universal Love for the entire human race, without
exception....Proclaim and publish to all the people of the
world a Universal Gospel that shall restore, in time, all
the human species....The inner Spirit makes us feel that
behind every appearance of diversity there is an
interdependent unity of all things."
George de Benneville (1703–1793)

"We must not look for religion in creeds or formularies of
human invention. We must look for it in the honest, the
pious, the devotional heart; in the heart which truly loves
God, loves its [sister and] brother also. The principle of love
to God and goodwill is true religion."
Hosea Ballou (1771–1852)

THANKS

Andrew would like to thank: John Morgan for the honour of writing this book with him; John Henson for the kind permission to use his translations of the New Testament; the congregation of the Memorial Church (Unitarian) Cambridge who called me to be their minister; Sabrina Lewins, John Coates and Jackie Metcalfe for teaching me so much about prayer; Gerry Metcalfe for his photograph; Dr Sophia Wellbeloved, Director of Lighthouse Editions for publishing this book and her general support, and the Unitarian Christian Association for financing it; the Revd Cliff Reed for inspiring me to follow a Unitarian Christian way of faith; Ali Parchami, Yvonne Cornish, Graham Driver, Victor Nuovo, Antonia Barke, Eric Eve and Andrew Perry for their friendship and support during my time in Oxford and since; the Revd Chris Wilson and his wife Sandra for their friendship and for being there at the toughest time in my own ministry; Mark Argent, not only for the cover design and general typographical advice, but also for his friendship; Joe Bord for his friendship and encouragement; my parents Alan and Pam Brown and my sister Helen for their unfailing love and support in all I have tried to do; and my musical colleagues and friends, Kevin Flanagan, Chris Ingham and Russ Morgan, who keep me grounded by reminding me that I am really just a jazz bass player. But most of all I would like to thank my wife, Susanna, without whom very little of this (or anything) would be possible. Her deep love and support continue to stun me.

John would like to express his thanks to Andrew who really was the organizer of the book. Without his involvement and that of the Unitarian Christian Association, this book might never have seen the light of day. Andrew and I worked as a team in the writing and there was a fundamental theological and spiritual unity between us which hopefully can be seen by the readers. I also want to thank the many, many Unitarian Universalists in congregations I have served over many decades of ministry who hunger for deeper spirituality. This book seeks to respond to those heartfelt needs. Just as the earliest Pietistic faith traditions in the U.S.A. grew by sub-dividing into small cells or conventicles, my hope is that this little book will encourage the formation of many small groups in the U.K. and U.S.A., for it is in this way that movements grow and deepen. Finally, having just come out of a long hospital stay in which I sometimes wondered if I would survive, I am more acutely aware than ever of life's preciousness and God's presence. I also am deeply aware of the love and support of family and friends, especially my wife, Cynthia, and my son, Jonathan, and daughters Lynne and Lori, with whom I am connected not only by blood but by spirit.

CONTENTS

INTRODUCTION

We offer this little book of prayers as a way to deepen your faith and the faith of others who may meet together in small groups, house churches or even occasional informal gatherings. We believe that there is a great hunger among those who call themselves disciples of Jesus, and those who seek to know him, to understand his life and teachings more deeply and apply these lessons to their own lives.

We believe that just as Jesus sought disciples among those who were outside the mainstream — tax collectors, women and fishermen — so, too, would he welcome those today who seek him reverently and earnestly, no matter their religious or philosophical inclinations. His is a living presence which encounters us in our depths.

We believe it is vital to a living faith to adopt a disciplined practice of daily prayer. Indeed, if we were really living as Jesus taught, our lives would themselves be a prayer because we would be in harmony with the will of God. But each one of us misses the mark and falls short of God's grace. That is why we need to be intentional about our devotional life, setting aside regular times for prayer and deep reflection, as we wake to a new day and as we prepare to rest for the night, as well as throughout all our waking moments.

Our heartfelt desire is to help you to begin or deepen your spiritual life — your connections to the Divine, your soul, and to others.

The underlying inspiration for this prayer book has been the Socinian/Unitarian, Universalist, Anabaptist, Mystical and Pietist traditions of the Radical Reformation which were the wellsprings from which sprang our own group of churches in both Great

Britain and the U.S.A. However, the prayers on pages twelve and thirteen are Unitarian Christian adaptations of prayers used by the *Brahmo Samaj* (*Society of God*). We share a creative two-century long relationship with this liberal Hindu reform movement and we can still learn much from their patterns of worship and daily devotion.

But, lying at the heart of this book is the creative encounter with Scripture which formed and shaped our forebears in every way imaginable. We need to meditate upon it and then, like them, take the lessons we discover there to heart and *live* them. However, it is important to understand that, in our daily devotional reading, we do not need to *agree* with every word we read for they are there as much to provoke us to critical thought as they are to calm and satisfy us. Like Jacob's struggle with God by the river Jabbok (Gen. 32), we must wrestle with the text, bringing to it our personal experiences and reason as well as the gentle but powerful insights of the radical liberal Christian tradition to which we belong. And so, each day begins and ends with scripture and prayer. There is space around each prayer so that you may note your own thoughts and prayers. It is not our intent to supplant your own language of the heart, but to encourage and enlarge its scope.

In the month of morning and evening prayers the quotations from scripture have all been taken from the King James Version (KJV) of the Bible of 1611. We realise that some people may find the decision to use this text unduly conservative but we think there are three good reasons for this. The first is that it gave English speaking people their own religious vocabulary and we wish to maintain a real connection with this. The second is that we believe it is important to remember always that the Biblical text is *not* a modern one and that it speaks to us from ages different in many ways from our own. Of course there was a time when the KJV was itself a modern translation but the passing of four hundred years has given us the rich fruit of historical distance. Thirdly, we have become aware that modern translations all too often try to make the text 'easier' to understand by narrowing down the range of possible interpretations which can be drawn from it. This is always a dangerous move because one of the greatest gifts of the Biblical text is precisely the *breadth* of possible interpretations that can be drawn from it. It is not a one-dimensional book but one in which human beings have tried to do the impossible — to speak of the infinite and eternal in terms of the finite and transient. We can only continue to access these infinite and eternal meanings when we allow the text to remain open to further interpretation so that more of God's light and truth may break forth from its words and the writers' experiences. In the *devotional* context it is a book which should be read spiritually and not literally.

We also believe with Dietrich Bonhoeffer, the martyred German pastor, that the spiritual life requires both solitude and community, "Let him who cannot be alone beware of community....Let him who is not in community beware of being alone....".[1] If people can be alone with themselves and with God, they are more likely to be at home with others because they already cherish the deeper life of the spirit. And if people are sensitive to their inner lives, they will be more in tune with the lives of others. For this reason, the book is divided into three sections: Part One contains a suggested pattern of daily private devotion (we also hope that this will be used as a pattern for community prayer); Part Two contains the

Lord's Prayer and morning and evening prayers for each day of the month; Part Three contains prayers and practices for small groups, house churches or other gatherings.

Every author writes with some audience in mind. We have certainly done so. Our intention has been to offer a spiritual resource for those who profess to be disciples of Jesus, and also for those who, as in days of old, wait around the fringe of the crowd, listening to his words and observing his behaviour. We hope that those who do not call themselves Christians may also find something of great value in the life and teachings of Jesus. Equally important, however, is that we have sought to create a resource that can be used by individuals for private devotions and for people gathered in small supportive groups, whether in house churches, prayer circles, or Bible study groups.

Lastly we wish to acknowledge two prayer books which have inspired and given us a format for this book: John Baillie's *A Diary of Private Prayer* (London & Toronto: Geoffrey Cumberlege, Oxford University Press, 1954); and *The Way of Prayer* (London: The Lindsey Press, 1960).

Andrew J. Brown
  Cambridge, England
John C. Morgan
  Reading, Pennsylvania
Easter 2007

1. Dietrich Bonhoeffer *Life Together*, New York: Harper and Row, 1954, p. 77
Note: We have chosen to use English rather than American spellings (i.e. "behaviour" rather than "behavior") for no other reason than that one of us is English and the other is from English and Welsh ancestry.

PART ONE
A PATTERN OF DAILY PRAYER

A PATTERN OF DAILY PRAYER

¶ *Begin by bringing yourself to silence (lighting a candle if you wish).† Then, either using traditional or modern language, say:*

Hear, O Israel: the Lord our God, the Lord is one; you shall love the Lord your God with all your heart, and with all your soul, and with all your mind, and with all your strength. And a second is like it: You shall love your neighbour as yourself. There is no other commandment greater than these. On these two commandments hang all the law and the prophets.

Mark 12:29–31; Matthew 22:40 (NRSV)

Or:

> The most important rule is, 'Listen, people of Israel. There is only one God. Love God with everything you have — your feelings, your intelligence, your physical strength.' The next most important rule is. 'Love the person next to you as you love yourself.' These are the most important rules. Everything else the rule books and God's speakers have to say is simply a working out of those two rules.
>
> *Mark 12:29–31; Matthew 22:40 (Henson)*

With what shall I come before the LORD, and bow myself before God on high? He has told you, O mortal, what is good; and what does the LORD require of you but to do justice, and to love kindness, and to walk humbly with your God?

Micah 6:6a, 8 (NRSV)

Our Father, who art in heaven, hallowed be thy name. Thy kingdom come. Thy will be done on earth, as it is in heaven. Give us this day our daily bread. And forgive us our trespasses, as we forgive those who trespass against us. And lead us not into temptation; but deliver us from evil. For thine is the kingdom, the power and the glory, for ever and ever. Amen.

Or:

> Loving God, here and everywhere, help us proclaim
> your values and bring in your New World. Supply us our
> day to day needs. Forgive us for wounding you, while
> we forgive those who wound us. Give us courage to
> meet life's trials and deal with evil's power. Amen.
>
> *(Henson)*

¶ *Reading/s. Here you may use the readings found in Part Two.*

¶ *A period of silent, meditative prayer on a verse or a word from your reading. Here you may also wish to use the daily prayers in Part Two.*

¶ *Prayer (praying as the Spirit moves you) but particularly on*
  Sunday: for all peoples and creation
  Monday: for family and friends
  Tuesday: for your church community
  Wednesday: for your village, town or city
  Thursday: for your country
  Friday: for the Church Invisible & Universal
  Saturday: for yourself

¶ *In the morning pray the Benedictus:*

Blessed be the Lord God of Israel, for he has looked favourably on his people and redeemed them. He has raised up a mighty saviour for us in the house of his servant David, as he spoke through the mouth of his holy prophets from of old, that we would be saved from our enemies and from the hand of all who hate us. Thus he has shown the mercy promised to our ancestors, and has remembered his holy covenant, the oath that he swore to our ancestor Abraham, to grant us that we, being rescued from the hands of our enemies, might serve him without fear, in holiness and righteousness before him all our days. And you, child, will be called the prophet of the Most High; for you will go before the Lord to prepare his ways, to give knowledge of salvation to his people by the forgiveness of their sins. By the tender mercy of our

8

God, the dawn from on high will break upon us, to give light to those who sit in darkness and in the shadow of death, to guide our feet into the way of peace.

Luke 1:68–79 (NRSV)

Or:

What a wonderful God, the God of Jacob, Leah, and Rachel! This God has come to help us and set us free. The world will be healed by the power of love, by a descendent of David and Bathsheba. Those who spoke God's promises were right: the days of hate and having enemies are passing. God was generous to our ancestors, a loyal and reliable friend. God pomised Abraham and Sarah an end to hostility and fear. Freedom to worship and serve. You, little baby, will speak for God; You will go in front of God's Chosen Leader and roll out the carpet. You'll tell the people their problems are over, free from guilt at last. God is kind and gentle; God will turn darkness into daylight, so we can make our way in peace.

Luke 1:68–79 (Henson)

¶ *In the evening pray the Magnificat:*

Mary said, "My soul magnifies the Lord, and my spirit rejoices in God my Saviour, for he has looked with favour on the lowliness of his servant. Surely, from now on all generations will call me blessed; for the Mighty One has done great things for me, and holy is his name. His mercy is for those who fear him from generation to generation. He has shown strength with his arm; he has scattered the proud in the thoughts of their hearts. He has brought down the powerful from their thrones, and lifted up the lowly; he has filled the hungry with good things, and sent the rich away empty. He has helped his servant Israel, in remembrance of his mercy, according to the promise he made to our ancestors, to Abraham and to his descendants forever."

Luke 1:46–55 (NRSV)

Or:

Mary said: I sense the greatness of God who makes my joy complete. God smiled at me and asked my help, and everyone will dance with glee at the wonderful thing happening to me. What a God! In every age God aids the good, upsetting the plans of the arrogant: See how the powerful fall off their perches! Honour for the modest, a banquet for the hungry; the rich get nothing and slink away! God keeps promises to friends and companions — Abraham, Sarah, and their like today.

Luke 1:46–55 (Henson)

¶ *In the morning pray the following or another prayer consecrating yourself to a life of faith as a disciple of Jesus Christ:*

Eternal God, who has committed to me the swift and solemn trust of life; since I know not what a day may bring forth, but only that the hour for serving You is always present, may I wake to the instant claims of Your holy will; not waiting for tomorrow, but yielding to-day. Lay to rest, by the persuasion of Your Spirit, the resistance of my passion, idleness, and fear. Consecrate with Your presence the way my feet may go; and the humblest work will shine, and the roughest places be made plain. Lift me above unrighteous anger and mistrust into faith and hope and love, by a simple and steadfast reliance on Your sure will: and so may I be modest in my time of wealth, patient under disappointment, ready for danger, serene in death. In all things, draw me to the mind of Christ, that Your lost image may be traced again, and You may own me as at one with him and You. Amen.

¶ *In the evening pray the following or another prayer:*

O Lord, our God, I come to You, the refuge of my soul, and in the quiet of this evening hour would rest under the shelter of Your love. Here, in communion with You, I would gain strength for the labours, patience for the trials, light for the perplexities and difficulties; and remembering my past failures, weakness and sin, humbly seek again the support and guidance which I have never yet trusted as I ought. I ask for Your forgiveness; and may I, in a holier spirit and with a more steadfast will, renounce the evil I lament and press forward in the way that leads to life and light. Amen.

¶ *In the morning conclude with the doxology from 1 Timothy or the Grace from 2 Corinthians:*

To the King of the ages, immortal, invisible, the only God, be honour and glory forever and ever. Amen.

1 Timothy 1:17 (NRSV)

The grace of our Lord Jesus Christ, the love of God, and the fellowship of the Holy Spirit be with us all, evermore. Amen.

2 Corinthians 13:14 (composite)

Or:

> May we know first-hand the beautiful character of our Leader, Jesus, God's Chosen, and the Love of God, and the special being together God's Spirit brings. Amen.

2 Corinthians 13:14 (Henson)

¶ *In the evening conclude with the Nunc Dimittus:*

Master, now you are dismissing your servant in peace, according to your word; for my eyes have seen your salvation, which you have prepared in the presence of all peoples, a light for revelation to the Gentiles and for glory to your people Israel. Amen.

Luke 2:29–32 (NRSV)

Or:

Your helper, God, moves on content, your plans my eyes have seen; a new day dawns for every land, beyond your people's dream. Amen.

Luke 2:29–32 (Henson)

¶ *End by resting in silence once more (and extinguishing the candle if you lit one).*

A PRAYER AT BATH

Loving God, this pure water, which refreshes, restores and cleans my body, is a special manifestation of Your love and care. It is a symbol of Your saving grace which purifies and strengthens the soul and so I give thanks for this most valued gift of Yours. As this water daily refreshes, restores and cleans my body so, too, may my soul be hallowed and strengthened by constant communion with You. I ask this in the spirit of Jesus, Amen.

A PRAYER BEFORE THE START OF WORK

Loving God, You are within and without me and, through my daily tasks and duties, You call me to loving service. May I always feel Your presence in the work I am going to begin. May Your wisdom enlighten and Your inspiration strengthen me and, when my energy and patience flag, may Your touch refresh and encourage me. Whenever I feel tempted to neglect my work or act carelessly, may I feel Your presence and be restored and steadied. Enable me to treat with kindness and compassion all with whom I may come into contact in the course of the day. Cure me of all selfish and ambitious desires, of the love of human applause, and enable me to seek only Your glory in all that I do. May my work, instead of separating my soul from You, draw me ever nearer and nearer to You and help my everlasting union with You. I ask this in the spirit of Jesus, Amen.

A GRACE AT MEALS

Eternal God, sustainer of all, I acknowledge that Your love and care is present in the food and drink before me and in every moment of its growth and preparation. With heartfelt gratitude I give thanks for this manifestation of Your love. May I always remember this with thankfulness, and use in Your service the health and strength gained through these Your gifts. I ask this in the spirit of Jesus, Amen.

A PRAYER BEFORE GOING TO BED

Loving God, after the labours of the day You have given me rest and invite me to resign all my thoughts and anxieties and fall asleep in the everlasting embrace of Your loving arms. I feel now Your love and my entire dependence upon You. Through sleep and waking, rest and labour, You fulfil Your holy will in my life and lead me on to my goal. After the blessed sleep You mercifully grant me, may I wake to a deepened consciousness of Your presence within and without me. I ask this in the spirit of Jesus, Amen.

† A few words on the lighting of a candle before prayer. If you choose to do it the authors encourage you to do this with intention, holding in your mind the flame as a symbol of the divine light that has come into the world and which no darkness can ever overcome (cf. John 1:5).

An almost forgotten radical, liberal Christian text which speaks profoundly of the symbolism of the candle was written by the Dutch Collegiant and advocate of Spinoza's philosophy, Peter Balling, entitled *The Light upon the Candlestick* (1663). The following short extracts from his pamphlet offer some powerful ideas upon which to meditate:

We direct thee then to within thyself, that is, that thou oughtest to turn into, to mind and have regard unto that which is within thee, to wit, The *Light* of Truth, the true *Light* which enlightens every man that cometh into the world. Here 'tis that thou must be, and not without thee....We say then, That we exhort every one to turn into the *Light*, that's in him *(We give it rather the appellation of Light, than any thing else, otherwise it's all one to us whether ye call it, Christ, the Spirit, the Word, &c. seeing these all denote but one and the same thing)*: Yet the word *Light* being in all its natural signification somewhat else then that which we intend thereby, we shall therefore in brief endeavour clearly to express what we intend under this denomination. *The Light* (then we say) *is a clear and distinct knowledge of truth in the understanding of every man, by which he is so convinced of the Being and Quality of things, that he cannot possibly doubt thereof.* From this definition which is here given of the *Light*, 'tis clear, that it must needs comprehend in it the principal effect of showing us, and giving us the knowledge of what's Truth and Falsehood, what's good and evil: which verily is a matter of so great concernment, that without it men must needs swerve up and down in continual darkness, opinion and sin, neither knowing truth at all, nor doing any good, but gropingly, by haphazard without any certainty. *This Light then, Christ the Truth, &c. is that which makes manifest and reproves sin in man, shewing him how he has strayed from God, accuseth him of the evil which he doth and hath committed; yea this is it which judgeth and condemeth him: Again, This is the preaching to every Creature under Heaven, though they have never read or heard of the Scripture. This is it which leads man into truth, into the way to God, which excuseth him in well-doing, giving him peace in his Conscience, yea, brings him into union with God, wherein all happiness and salvation doth consist....The Light is also the first Principle of Religion.* For seeing there can be no true Religion without the knowledge of God, and no knowledge of God without this *Light*, Religion must necessarily have this *Light* for its first Principle.

PART TWO
THE LORD'S PRAYER
MORNING AND EVENING PRAYERS
A PLAN FOR INDIVIDUAL RETREATS

THE LORD'S PRAYER

Jesus taught this prayer to all those beginning in the life of the Spirit. In so doing, he was not so much teaching us words to be used unchangingly, but instead a *pattern* of how to pray. In the King James translation of Matthew (6:9) and Luke (11:12) we read that Jesus simply told us we should pray *after this manner* or *like* this.

In his prayer Jesus calls us, firstly, to name and honour God and then to ask that God's perfect eternal way is reflected in our own transient lives and communities. Next, we are to ask for that which we truly *need* rather than that which we merely *want*. Then, Jesus calls upon us to ask for forgiveness of ourselves and others and, lastly, that we may have the wisdom to choose the good ways so that we are not led into temptations or influenced by evil. Matthew's version of the prayer finishes with a shout of praise to God's ultimate unity in which all things live and move and have their being.

Of course we should not forget nor cease to use the pattern prayer of Jesus in the manner we have learnt it but, as we do this, we should not forget that his basic purpose was to encourage us to create our own living prayers — to speak directly to God in the language of our own hearts. Just as we are encouraging you to replace the daily prayers which follow with your own, we also encourage you to shape and pray your own prayer according to the pattern Jesus offered us. On the following page are just two possibilities:

Abba, parent of us all, may Your name be hallowed and Your perfection mirrored in our own lives and world. Each day may we have enough food to sustain us in lives of loving service. Forgive us when we fail You as we forgive those who fail us. Strengthen us to choose the good ways and to avoid those which harm Your creation. You are to us all goodness, all strength and all wonder. Amen.

Holy One who art everywhere but close at hand, may Your kingdom come, Your will be done, on earth and in eternity. Give us every day our daily needs. Forgive us our shortcomings, as we forgive the shortcomings of others. Help us to resist temptation; keep us from evil. For Yours is the kingdom, now and forever. Amen.

A MONTH OF
MORNING AND EVENING PRAYERS

DAY 1 — THE ALL-PERVADING GOD

Morning

Whither shall I go from thy spirit or whither shall I flee from thy presence? If I ascend up into heaven, thou art there: if I make my bed in hell, behold, thou art there. If I take the wings of the morning, and dwell in the uttermost parts of the sea; Even there shall thy hand lead me, and thy right hand shall hold me.

Psalm 139:7–10 (KJV)

Eternal and Loving God, in this time of prayer as I prepare to enter the busy world once more, may I come to know that there is no place in this world, nor any place in my own heart, where You are not present; no place where Your hands are not outstretched in love ready to lead and hold me. In all that I see and do today, teach me to understand ever more deeply that only in You do all things live and move and have their being.

May I also come to understand that, as Your eternal presence knows no restrictions of place it also knows none of time, and so Your voice may be discerned across all history and peoples.

Holding all these thoughts in my heart today may Your eternal presence within and without me, in and through all things, guide my heart and hands in this and every day's work.

These things I ask in the spirit of Jesus whose disciple I seek to be. Amen.

DAY 1 — THE ALL-PERVADING GOD

Evening

Jesus said: "Father, into thy hands I commend my spirit"

Luke 23:46 (KJV)

O God, as I come to the end of this day and give myself up into the embrace of Your ever-loving arms, I ask forgiveness for the times I lost sight of Your eternal presence in and around me and so acted apart from Your guiding and sustaining Love.

Despite my failings I recall, with grateful thanks and praise, the times when I felt Your presence as a living spirit which guided me to a more perfect service of You and my neighbours. In those moments I knew, as Jesus taught, that the kingdom of Heaven is present within and that You are closer to me than my own heartbeat.

So now, acknowledging that as the day is Yours so, too, is the night, with Jesus I say, "Father, into thy hands I commend my spirit." Amen.

DAY 2 — THE PRAYERFUL LIFE

Morning

The day is thine, the night also is thine: thou hast prepared the light and the sun. Thou hast set all the borders of the earth: thou hast made summer and winter.

Psalm 74:16–17 (KJV)

God of all times and seasons, of morning and night, who is as close to me as my own breathing yet as deeply mysterious as the many universes I intuit but never see, I come before You acknowledging Your love for me, even when I have sinned and fallen short of Your commandment to love You and my neighbour as myself. In the light of day, I confess my shortcomings but I know that in bringing them to You I am forgiven and made ready to begin anew.

As I begin this day, keep me mindful that You stay with me, that You know my comings and my goings, my joys and my sorrows. Instil in me a renewed sense of Your presence in my life, from the first signs of self to the eternal now. Let me not forget You, God, lest I lose myself in the day and remember not Your blessings.

I ask these things in the name of Jesus, my brother, who said You would never abandon those You love and call by name. Amen.

Evening

And [Jesus] spake a parable unto them to this end, that men ought always to pray, and not to faint.

Luke 18:1 (KJV)

O God, I have cried unto You for deliverance from my sufferings, from the pain I cause others, and from the tribulations of those who would do me harm. I grow weary. I do not always feel You beside me. As I enter the night, keep me safe and in Your care. Comfort me with the sure knowledge that You have not forsaken me, even when I do not sense Your hand in mine.

Now as day ends, I will enter sleep trusting in Your mercy, knowing that even when I struggle and faint, You have not left me alone. Amen.

DAY 3 — THE UNFAILING COMPANION

Morning

The LORD is my light and my salvation; whom shall I fear? the LORD is the strength of my life; of whom shall I be afraid? Wait on the LORD: be of good courage, and he shall strengthen thine heart: wait I say on the LORD.

Psalm 27:1, 14 (KJV)

Eternal God, give me a trustful spirit so that in all I do, I may come to know You are unfailingly by my side, the perfect companion of the Way.

Many times Your morning light has revealed to me the safe paths upon which to walk, and on them I have been accompanied by the innumerable wonders of Your creation: the birds of the air; the flowers of the field; the hills and valleys; rivers and seas. Their beauty inspires my being and dispels my fears. May I also come to know more fully that Your light reveals, too, an inner landscape and shows me ever more perfect ways my heart should walk.

In all my journeyings, both outer and inner, may I have strength and courage to call upon You with the same trust and patience as did my Teacher, the Rabbi Jesus, and so discover that Your saving and guiding Word eternally companions me on all the paths of my life. Amen.

DAY 3 — THE UNFAILING COMPANION

Evening

Jesus said: Your Father knoweth what things ye
have need of, before ye ask him.
Matthew 6:8 (KJV)

Lord, as I have given thanks for the light of the day
now passing, I begin to give thanks for Your gift of
night. Too often I have feared the coming of the
evening hours but, trusting in Your wisdom and
perfect knowledge, teach me that there is a divine
purpose to be found in Your gift of darkness, and that
I have need of its healing grace. In darkness You
renew my body, mind and spirit and bring to birth all
things. Your darkness never obscures but only reveals
more of Your creative and loving presence. As the
sunlight fades, the appearance of the starry heavens
above is yet another sign to me of Your
companioning presence throughout all creation.
Amen.

DAY 4 — GOD IS GOOD

Morning

The LORD is my shepherd; I shall not want. He maketh me to lie down in green pastures: He leadeth me beside the still waters. He restoreth my soul...Surely goodness and mercy shall follow me all the days of my life: And I will dwell in the house of the LORD for ever.

Psalm 23:1–3, 6 (KJV)

Good and Gracious God, help me to see the goodness of creation, the starry heavens above and the moral law within. Sustain in me a trusting heart; stifle the doubts about the transitory nature of life and the dangers of living. Keep fresh within me the joy of life, the feeling of its power and synergy, the love of all life's creatures. O God, You never said that creation was perfect, but the inner light of Your wisdom planted deep within our souls reveals to me its good purposes, its perfect imperfection which draws out of me acts of true love and service. Lead me beside still waters. Encourage me to lie down in green pastures. Restore my soul. And I will dwell in Your house for ever. Amen.

DAY 4 — GOD IS GOOD

Evening

Jesus asked: Why callest thou me good? None is good, save one, that is, God.

Luke 18:19 (KJV)

As the daylight fades, O Holy One, I come unto You, trusting in Your goodness and mercy toward me. I confess the shortcomings of my day and the acts of kindness I have sometimes failed to show. As I enter the silence of night, Lord, help me to rest easy and feel restored when the morning light breaks again, knowing You are good. Amen.

DAY 5 — FOLLOWING THE WAY

Morning

Fret not thyself because of evildoers, neither be thou envious against the workers of iniquity. For they shall soon be cut down like the grass, and wither as the green herb. Trust in the LORD, and do good; so shalt thou dwell the land, and verily thou shalt be fed. Delight thyself also in the LORD; and he shall give thee the desires of thine heart. Commit thy way unto the LORD; trust also in him; and he shall bring it to pass.

Psalm 37:1–5 (KJV)

O God, as I begin this day, I acknowledge that I will know times of hardship and difficulty. But in those times, may I remember I have committed myself to Your Way and that, whatever evil or danger faces or befalls me, I have come to know that Your goodness and love is greater than them all. May I remember to trust in You and to do only good, never turning aside in envy or fear. May I have the strength and courage to delight in You as on those days when all about me, I saw only light, love and beauty. I ask these things in the spirit of him who walked Your Way faithfully through all the joys and vicissitudes of life, the Rabbi Jesus. Amen.

DAY 5 — FOLLOWING THE WAY

Evening

Jesus said: I am the way, the truth, and the life: no man cometh unto the Father, but by me.

John 14:6 (KJV)

Eternal, Loving and Wise God, teach me to understand that those who perfectly follow Your precepts become themselves Your Way. In the life of Jesus I have witnessed such perfect devotion and so seen the Way, the Truth and the Life. I know that I cannot truly come unto You unless I, too, follow Your perfect path with all my heart, mind and soul. May this night of rest refresh and strengthen me so that I awake ready to follow the example of Jesus in the holy pilgrimage of life. Amen.

DAY 6 — GOD IS LOVE

Morning

O praise the LORD, all ye nations: praise him, all ye people. For his merciful kindness is great toward us: and the truth of the LORD endureth for ever. Praise ye the LORD.

Psalm 117 (KJV)

Lover of my soul, God of kindness, I come before You this morning knowing my weaknesses and all too aware of my shortcomings, but also humbly aware of Your promise not to forsake me. O God, I suffer when I realize how little I have done to advance Your kingdom, how often I have walked past those who needed my help, how seldom I pay attention to Your voice within calling me to the greater good. I ask You to forgive me, even as I know I must seek forgiveness from those I have wounded, however deep my resistance. Lord, have mercy upon me. Lord, cleanse my spirit of all evil thoughts and selfish motives. Lord, forgive me and let me begin the day knowing of Your steadfast love, that I may forgive myself and others and be free. So be it.

DAY 6 — GOD IS LOVE

Evening

Jesus said unto him, "Thou shalt love the LORD thy God with all thy heart, and with all thy soul, and with all thy mind." This is the first and great commandment. And the second is like unto it, "Thou shalt love thy neighbour as thyself." On these two commandments hang all the law and prophets.

Matthew 22:37–40 (KJV)

As the evening light fades away, I pray that Your law will be planted in my heart where it will never leave me. I seek to love You, God, with all my strength, and to love my neighbour as I love myself. I may fall short, O God, but I gather hope knowing that when I fall, You will help me rise to my feet and begin again. I may find it hard to love those who hurt me, but I know that Your command to love others requires me to see one of Your children even in my supposed enemy. Bless me, O Lord, now and in the coming night and day, that I may truly be called Your disciple. I pray in the name of Jesus who showed us how to love. Amen.

DAY 7 — THE DIVINE GLORY

Morning

And suddenly there was with the angel a multitude of the heavenly host praising God, and saying, Glory to God in the highest, and on earth peace, good will toward men.

Luke 2:13–14 (KJV)

Ever creative and gracious God, may the appearance of Your Divine Glory surprise me into seeking new life this day. Let me not be seduced by the merely grand or dramatic, but instead recall that I have most often glimpsed the homeland of the spirit in the ordinary moments of life: in the freely offered smile, hand and word. May these ordinary, divine messengers come to me as they did to the wise teachers of old, enabling me to see the birth of the extraordinary in the midst of the ordinary. Teach me always to be awake and ready to receive these holy gifts and through them grow into a deeper appreciation, reverence and love of You and Your world. But let me not only receive, teach me also to be an open door through which Your Glory may pass to lighten our darkness. May it be so.

DAY 7 — THE DIVINE GLORY

Evening

Glory in his holy name; let the hearts of those who seek the LORD rejoice! Seek the LORD and his strength, seek his presence continually! Remember the wonderful works that he has done, his miracles, and the judgments he uttered.

Psalm 105:3–5 (KJV)

O Lord God, as the time of stillness and rest approaches let me come unto You as one who rejoices in Your Divine Glory and Name. I remember now all Your wonderful works and judgments; those that I have seen in my own life and those my forebears bequeathed to me in the ancient stories of my faith.

In my memories of Your gracious dealings with me and Your people and, in calling upon Your Holy Name, I bring myself to rest in Your presence. Amen.

DAY 8 — OUR LIKENESS TO GOD

Morning

As for me, I will behold thy face in righteousness: I shall be satisfied, when I awake, with thy
likeness.

Psalm 17:15 (KJV)

O God, sometimes I have felt You were so distant that
I might never reach You. I yearn to reach out and
touch the stars so that I may discover Your presence
in creation, but I know my desire exceeds my reach. I
read the stories others have written of Your mighty
acts in history, but they seem long ago and in times I
do not fully understand. I listen for You when others
speak, but I hear only their words. I try to sense Your
presence in music and art, and the great works of
literature, but these are the feelings of others, not
mine. I walk in the woods and behold the sky and
trees and flowers and know they bear Your imprint
and yet still I am not satisfied. I hunger for You but I
am not filled. Where shall I go to find You; to what
heights or depths must I travel before I see You?

Then I understand! Then I awake satisfied! For You
have planted this hunger deep within me so that
nothing finite will suffice, but only Your likeness in
me which is as close to me as my breath, as near as
my own beating heart, always present in this moment
of time and space. So be it.

DAY 8 — OUR LIKENESS TO GOD

Evening

Jesus said: My mother and my brethren are these which hear the word of God, and do it.

Luke 8:21 (KJV)

Help me to listen, Lord, to Your voice within, calling me to love mercy and do justice and walk humbly in my chosen path. Stifle the rehearsed response, the measured deed, the outward signs of piety. Teach me to hear and behave by the light You have given me, which is to love others and myself for You have sown within me a garden of life. As I fall into sleep, let me rest assured of Your presence in my heart, where it will remain, in this life and in the next. Amen.

DAY 9 — REBIRTH

Morning

Jesus said: That which is born of the flesh is flesh; and that which is born of the Spirit is spirit. Marvel not that I said unto thee, ye must be born again. The wind bloweth where it listeth, and thou hearest the sound thereof, but canst not tell whence it cometh, and whither it goeth: so is every one that is born of the Spirit.

John 3:6–8 (KJV)

Eternal God, as I awake this morning, I pray that I may be born anew in Your Spirit. Teach me to trust its surprising movements and allow its creative wisdom to guide all my actions. In the moment of inspiration, let me not come to despise or undervalue the created world but instead see it as a visible sign of Your invisible eternal presence. May my rebirth in Your Spirit reveal to me that everything in this world is truly a precinct of the kingdom of Heaven and that here there is nothing lacking. I ask these things in the name of Jesus who, filled with Your presence, surprised those he met into a new way of life. Amen.

DAY 9 — REBIRTH

Evening

And he hath put a new song in my mouth, even praise unto our God: many shall see it, and fear, and shall trust in the LORD. Blessed is that man that maketh the LORD his trust, and respecteth not the proud, nor such as turn aside to lies. Many, O LORD my God, are thy wonderful works which thou hast done, and thy thoughts which are to us-ward: they cannot be reckoned up in order unto thee: if I would declare and speak of them, they are more than can be numbered.

Psalm 40:3–5 (KJV)

O Divine Comforter, I give thanks for all the things which, today, I have undertaken in the new life of the Spirit. I ask forgiveness, too, for all the things which were not done in this new spirit and where I brought harm, no matter how small, instead of healing.

But, above all, I come unto You now with new songs of thanksgiving and praise for I know that, despite my repeated failings fully to be reborn in the Spirit of love, You will never abandon me if I truly seek to remake myself in imitation of Your perfection. May I rest secure in the knowledge that Your desire for me is only to have life and to have it more abundantly. I ask these things in the universal, ever new and healing spirit revealed to me in Jesus. Amen.

DAY 10 — OVERCOMING FEAR

Morning

Yea, though I walk through the valley of the shadow of death, I will fear no evil: for Thou art with me...."

Psalm 23:4 (KJV)

O God, in Your presence, where I am already known, I dare not hide my fear of living and of dying. I fear how risky life is and how small I am. I fear being overcome with losses so that I fear life itself. Most of all I fear dying and death because I do not know for certain what is beyond. All my achievements, all my friends and family, all that I love in this life might be taken from me in the blink of an eye. Yet, God, I also know that if I lean on You, I will not be forsaken; if I call on You, my voice will be heard. Yet how difficult it is for me to trust Your promise that I will not be forsaken. Help me, Lord, to trust more and fear less, to fret less and listen more, to understand that You know who I am and where I am going. Amen.

DAY 10 — OVERCOMING FEAR

Evening

And there arose a great storm of wind, and the waves beat into the ship, so that it was now full. And [Jesus] was in the hinder part, asleep on a pillow; and they awake him, and say unto him, "Master, carest thou not that we perish?" And he arose and rebuked the wind, and said unto the sea, "Peace, be still." And the wind ceased, and there was a great calm. And he said unto them, "Why are ye so fearful? How is it that you have no faith?"

Mark 4:37–40 (KJV)

As I prepare for sleep, O God, I pray to feel deep within me a great calm because I know that whether I am awake or sleeping, You are never far away. Though I fear death, You will save me; though I fear how brief and tenuous life is, You have promised that neither life nor death will take me away from Your love. Let a great calming peace descend now in my heart so that when I awake, I will not be afraid. Amen.

DAY 11 — IDENTITY AND BELONGING

Morning

Jesus said: If two of you shall agree on earth as touching any thing that they shall ask, it shall be done for them of my Father which is in heaven. For where two or three are gathered together in my name, there am I in the midst of them.

Matthew 18:19–20 (KJV)

God of all belonging, may Jesus' words remind me that I am called upon, not only to be a solitary seeker of Your wisdom, but to seek it in community. You have taught me that the kingdom of Heaven is a reality within my own heart, but let me not forget that there it is but the seed of Your divine promise. Remind me that it is amongst my brothers and sisters that this seed must be sown. When two or three of us gather in Your name a beautiful flower grows which gives fragrance to our lives and our world. So today, help me to have courage openly and gently to seek out others who might come to share Your vision of a Bright New World. Together, we shall discover that we belong to You alone and will come to know who we truly are — Your own sons and daughters. Amen.

Evening

The LORD is the portion of mine inheritance and of my cup: thou maintainest my lot. The lines are fallen unto me in pleasant places; yea, I have a goodly heritage. I will bless the LORD, who hath given me counsel: my reins also instruct me in the night seasons. I have set the LORD always before me: because he is at my right hand, I shall not be moved. Therefore my heart is glad, and my glory rejoiceth: my flesh also shall rest in hope.

Psalm 16:5–9 (KJV)

Eternal and Loving God, as I reflect upon the day, with all the frustrations bequeathed to me by present circumstances and birth, may I come to understand that without boundaries and heritage I cannot know who I am, nor what it is I must do. Teach me to see my whole life as a goodly heritage inspiring me to greater faith and service. Tonight, let me simply give myself up to Your counsel. I trust that You will speak to my soul as I rest and that Your divine Word will be a sure rein, guiding me to my true place of belonging. Then, in the true light of Your kingdom's perfect dawn, I will finally see that throughout my life the lines had indeed fallen to me in pleasant places. So now, as I come into Your presence to rest in hope, my heart is glad and I rejoice. Amen.

DAY 12 — JOY

Morning

Make a joyful noise unto the LORD, all ye lands.
Serve the LORD with gladness: come before his
presence with singing. Know ye that the LORD
he is God: It is he that hath made us, and not
we ourselves; we are his people, and the sheep
of his pasture. Enter into his gates with
thanksgiving, and into his courts with praise:
Be thankful unto him, and bless his name. For
the LORD is good; his mercy is everlasting; and
his truth endureth to all generations.

Psalm 100 (KJV)

God of the morning light, I pray that during my
waking hours I will not let any anxiety or fear or
sadness stand in the way of finding You in the
presence of nature or others or within myself. Let me
look forward to this day joyfully, appreciating the
experiences which are before me, welcoming gifts of
love and kindness. Whatever I do today, let me not
forget Your lovingkindness to me. Somewhere today,
let laughter heal my soul and thanksgiving my heart.
Amen.

DAY 12 — JOY

Evening

Jesus said: How think ye? If a man have an hundred sheep, and one of them be gone away, doth he not leave the ninety and nine, and goeth into the mountains, and seeketh that which is gone astray? And if so be that he find it, verily I say unto you, he rejoiceth more of that sheep than of the ninety and nine which went not astray. Even so it is not the will of your Father which is in heaven, that one of these little ones perish.

Matthew 18:12–14 (KJV)

Forgiving Presence, which welcomes everyone back to Your community, I thank You for my new life. I know I have fallen short of Your glory. I know that whatever others think of me, I have often thought too highly of myself and too little of others. I understand all too well my own shortcomings and try as I might, I never seem entirely to rid myself of them. Thank You for accepting me when I had a hard time accepting myself. In humility I promise to live as You will and not as I want. As the light fades and night descends I send a prayer of joyful thanksgiving to You. Amen.

DAY 13 — TRUTH

Morning

Mercy and truth are met together; righteousness and peace have kissed each other. Truth shall spring out of the earth; and righteousness shall look down from heaven.

Psalm 85:10–11 (KJV)

O God, in the love of Truth and the Spirit of Jesus I wake this morning ready to serve my brothers and sisters and to worship You. I give thanks that the certainty of Your love, mercy and justice fills my heart and guides my heart and hands, soul and mind. But, even as You guide me in my actions today, remind me that Your eternal Truths are seen in this world only in part — as in a glass darkly. To me is not given certainty of belief but only the certainty of faith. So, in witnessing to Your abiding Truth, may I always remain open to new light and be prepared to change my beliefs that I may save my faith. Amen.

DAY 13 — TRUTH

Evening

Then said Jesus to those Jews which believed on him, "If ye continue in my word, then are ye my disciples indeed; And ye shall know the truth, and the truth shall make you free."

John 8:31–32 (KJV)

For the times I knew Your Truth but failed to act with love, mercy and justice in my heart, I ask now for Your forgiveness.

For the times Truth ran through me as a living stream informing all I said and did, I give joyful thanks.

May the sleep of this night restore my strength to continue to seek Your True Word which Jesus promised would make me free. Amen.

DAY 14 — REST AND RENEWAL

Morning

The LORD is thy keeper: the LORD is thy shade
upon thy right hand. The sun shall not smite
thee by day, nor the moon by night. The LORD
shall preserve thee from all evil; He shall
preserve thy soul. The LORD shall preserve thy
going out and thy coming in from this time
forth, and even for evermore.

Psalm 121:5–8 (KJV)

Keeper of my days, preserve my going out and my
coming in so that my soul may find rest and be
renewed. Around me I sense a thousand demands
upon my life so that I feel drained even before
beginning a new day. Keep Your light in my heart
that I may remember Your presence always and face
the day before me with courage, hope, and assurance
that I do not walk alone. May it be so. Amen.

DAY 14 — REST AND RENEWAL

Evening

And the apostles gathered themselves together unto Jesus, and told him all things, both what they had done, and what they had taught. And he said unto them, "Come ye yourselves apart into a desert place, and rest a while," for there were many coming and going, and they had no leisure so much as to eat.

Mark 6:30–31 (KJV)

Jesus said: I will not leave you comfortless: I will come to you. Yet a little while, and the world seeth me no more; but ye shall see me; because I live, ye shall live also. At that day ye shall know that I am in my Father, and you in me, and I in you.

John 14:18–20 (KJV)

O God, as I prepare to be renewed by sleep, I would let today's troubles flee my mind so that my spirit may find rest in You. I remember the promise of Jesus: that his burden is light and his faith strong. In Your will is my strength; in Your promise of continuing presence is my calm repose. In the gathering night, I trust in Your care. In the name of one who lives still. Amen.

DAY 15 — THE CALL TO FORGIVE

Morning

Jesus said: If ye forgive men their trespasses, your heavenly Father will also forgive you: But if ye forgive not men their trespasses, neither will your Father forgive your trespasses.

Matthew 6:14–15 (KJV)

Abba, Father, may my whole being this day remain aware of Your loving and forgiving nature. As I step out into the world may I recall that, as I am made in Your image, I am called upon to manifest Your love and forgiveness through my own life. Help me to follow the example of Jesus who taught us to forgive even those who seek to take our lives. May his extraordinary act remind me that so much of what I must forgive is of far less import, and that my failure to forgive continually holds me back from becoming a true force for good in this world. Let today be filled with forgiveness. Amen.

DAY 15 — THE CALL TO FORGIVE

Evening

Be merciful unto me, O LORD: for I cry unto thee daily. Rejoice the soul of thy servant: for unto thee, O LORD, do I lift up my soul. For thou, LORD, art good, and ready to forgive; and plenteous in mercy unto all them that call upon thee. Give ear, O LORD, unto my prayer; and attend to the voice of my supplications. In the day of my trouble I will call upon thee: for thou wilt answer me.

Psalm 86:3–7 (KJV)

Merciful God, I know that even when I try my best I cannot avoid actions which will require me to ask for Your forgiveness and the forgiveness of others. May I not forget that my knowledge is always partial and that what seems good and righteous now may seem, in time, to have been wrong. Give me the courage not to cease trying to live and act according to Your will, for You have promised that if I forgive others, You will hear me when I call upon You for forgiveness and mercy. May this knowledge free me to act more lovingly, more justly and more creatively in Your world, and so come to sleep, each and every night, in peace and confidence. Amen.

DAY 16 — DON'T LOSE HEART

Morning

I will praise thee, for thou hast heard me, and art become my salvation. The stone which the builders refused is become the head stone of the corner. This is the LORD's doing; it is marvellous in our eyes. This is the day which the LORD hath made; we will rejoice and be glad in it.

Psalm 118:21–24 (KJV)

O God, let me not grow faint from my troubles or the suffering of the world. As I begin a new day, keep fresh before me Your presence, that I may remember to whom I am committed and what You require of me: To love mercy, do justice, and walk humbly with You. Help me to see that what the world may consider insignificant becomes ultimate in Your sight. Let me see rejection not as defeat but only a temporary roadblock. Renew in me the sure knowledge that the coming day belongs to You, which You have given me to live well and serve others. Let me rejoice and be glad. So be it.

DAY 16 — DON'T LOSE HEART

Evening

Jesus said: There was in a city a judge, which feared not God, neither regarded man. And there was a widow in that city, and she came to him, saying, "Avenge me of my adversary." And he would not for a while; but afterward he said within himself, "Though I fear not God nor regard man, Yet because this woman troubleth me, I will avenge her, lest by her continual coming she weary me."

Luke 18:2–5 (KJV)

Lord, hear my cry for justice in the midst of my troubles. I do not always understand why I must suffer in body, mind or spirit. There are days I feel You are not there, that You do not listen; so I cry out loudly within: God, rescue me from this body of death, save me from my inner torments, release me from the clutches of those who would do me harm. I fear that You grow weary of my complaints, yet still I bring them. Hear me, God, that in the hearing alone I know I have been heard. Let me not lose heart in Your justice, so that Your will, not mine, may be done. I pray this in the name of a man who knew suffering and yet still sought to do thy will. Amen.

DAY 17 — TRUE PEACE

Morning

Jesus said: Suppose ye that I am come to give peace on earth? I tell you, Nay; but rather division: For from henceforth there shall be five in one house divided, three against two, and two against three.

Luke 12:51–52 (KJV)

God of True Peace, give me the wisdom to understand, as did Jesus, that to be Your witness on earth is always to challenge the unjust and violent whose response has always been to turn unjustly and violently upon the innocent. Despite this fearful reality may I, like the Prince of Peace himself, continually seek peace on earth, and so come to inherit the true everlasting peace which is Your kingdom. I ask for the deep courage and strength to speak and act for True Peace even when it reveals deep divisions existing within my own family, my own household of faith, and my own country. May I come to realize that only by working for a true and lasting peace on earth will the everlasting unity, for which my heart yearns, come to pass. Amen.

DAY 17 — TRUE PEACE

Evening

Pray for the peace of Jerusalem: they shall prosper that love thee. Peace be within thy walls, and prosperity within thy palaces. For my brethren and companions' sakes, I will now say, Peace be within thee.

Psalm 122:6–8 (KJV)

O God, Lord of Peace and Justice, in Your holy presence tonight, may I glimpse again a vision of the heavenly city of Jerusalem surrounded, not with divisive walls of concrete and barbed wire, but with the permeable yet protective walls of Your universal love. You have promised that within this city, Your own heart of hearts, there is true peace and prosperity for everyone, regardless of all which once divided one person from another. Jesus taught us that the entrance to this city, Your kingdom, lies within and so, tonight, in my prayers may I come closer to its welcoming doors. May my glimpses of its skyline so assure me of the reality of this heavenly Jerusalem, that with confidence I can say to all earthly Jerusalems, "Peace be within thee," and begin to play my part in their journey towards everlasting peace. Amen.

DAY 18 — SIN

Morning

Such as sit in darkness and in the shadow of death, being bound in affliction and iron, because they had rebelled against the word of God.

Psalm 107:10–11 (KJV)

O God, I know I am more like other people than I care to admit, that I rebel against Your inward laws daily, that I put myself first and You a distant second. Let me begin a new day confessing how far I fall short of Your wishes for me, how I do what You would not wish and neglect the most important tasks of loving You and my neighbour as myself.

Cleanse me today of all self-serving thoughts and motivations that lead only to my own best interests without considering those of others. Lord, You know I fail; I cannot hide from Your watchful eye nor escape Your listening ear. Have mercy on me as I confess my sins and seek the strength to change and move on. Amen.

DAY 18 — SIN

Evening

Jesus said: But those things which proceed out of the mouth come forth from the heart, and they defile the man. For out of the heart proceed evil thoughts.

Matthew 15:18–19 (KJV)

But that ye may know that the Son of Man hath power on earth to forgive sins.

Mark 2:10 (KJV)

God, I come before You at the close of day knowing that nothing can be hidden. I come as I am, understanding my lack of compassion toward others, my need to justify myself before all else, my failure to serve You in word and deed. I know myself as I am, not as others think I am, but only You see me as I truly am, not as I wish myself to be. I also know You are slow to anger and forgiving of those who confess their sins. In the name of Jesus, who forgave even those who crucified him, I ask Your forgiveness. And I pledge in God's strength, I will rise tomorrow with renewed hope and purpose to serve You. So be it.

Morning

He is the LORD our God: his judgments are in all the earth. He hath remembered his covenant for ever, the word which he commanded to a thousand generations. Which covenant he made with Abraham.

Psalm 105:7–9 (KJV)

All the paths of the LORD are mercy and truth unto such as keep his covenant and his testimonies.

Psalm 25:10 (KJV)

God of perfect promise, I am grateful to belong to a people who have a lasting Covenant with You. May I never forget that I share this Covenant with my Jewish and Muslim brothers and sisters. In keeping to Your paths as a faithful disciple of the Rabbi Jesus, help me to bring mercy, truth and respect into my all encounters with the many children of Abraham.

But, in my gratefulness at Your special Covenant with us, let me not forget that in Your love and mercy, You have made other Covenants of faith and they, too, will be lasting and trustworthy. With the people of these Covenants may I find common ground in building a world of peace and justice. Amen.

DAY 19 — GOD'S COVENANT

Evening

And [Jesus] took bread, and gave thanks, and brake it, and gave unto them, saying, "This is my body which is given for you: this do in remembrance of me." Likewise also the cup after supper, saying, "This cup is the new testament [or covenant] in my blood, which is shed for you."

Luke 22:19–20 (KJV)

God of new promise, through my sharing of bread and wine with all those who seek to be disciples of Jesus, renew in me tonight a sense of belonging to You. Remind me not to stumble over external forms and to understand that bread and wine can also be shared in the actions of the heart and spirit; communion with You is both an inner and outer reality. This remembrance and reconnection with Your presence and promise sustains me in all I do and it has revealed to me that I am not alone but a true child of Your great family. In Jesus I have seen and understood the Covenant You have made with all humankind. Let this be enough to sustain me to the end of this, and all my days. Amen.

DAY 20 — LIFE EVERLASTING

Morning

Return unto thy rest, O my soul, for the LORD hath dealt bountifully with thee. For thou hast delivered my soul from death, mine eyes from tears, and my feet from falling. I will walk before the LORD in the land of the living.

Psalm 116:7–9 (KJV)

Yea, though I walk through the valley of the shadow of death, I will fear no evil, for thou art with me.

Psalm 23:4 (KJV)

O God, as I start the day, I call to mind all those I love who have departed this life, and name them in my heart (*offer names*). O God, I miss them more than words can say. They remain with me, brought to consciousness in words I remember them saying, in places we have been together, and in times shared. The losses sometimes leave me empty and sorrowful. Lord, I do know how long I have in life's sojourn, yet I know You have called me to the land of the living for some tasks, great or small, that will glorify Your name on earth. As I walk through the day, God, grant me the inner knowledge that You will never leave alone those You love, but bring them into Your presence, until that day when all those who love You will be home. Though the veil which separates me from those who have parted this life seems so dense, lift it from time to time that I may see. Amen.

Evening

And [a young man] saith unto them, "Be not affrighted. Ye seek Jesus of Nazareth, which was crucified. He is not here; behold the place where they laid him."

Mark 16:6 (KJV)

Jesus said unto [Martha], "I am the resurrection and the life. He that believeth in me, though he were dead, yet shall he live. And whosoever liveth and believeth in me shall never die. Believest thou this?"

John 11:25–26 (KJV)

I do not know the day or hour of my departure from this earth, any more than I planned my entrance into it. I only know, O God, that where You art, there I shall be with You.

Love is more powerful than death, more enduring than my days on earth, more certain than all my doubts. I will rest now, trusting in Your promise not to forsake or leave me, not to abandon me to dust, not to forget my name. I am more than victor through him who has called me into his presence. I await the day of homecoming with all those I love, and at the feet of Jesus. Make it so, Lord. Amen.

DAY 21 — GATHERING UP

Morning

And Jesus took the loaves; and when he had
given thanks, he distributed to the disciples,
and the disciples to them that were set down;
and likewise of the fishes as much as they
would. When they were filled, he said unto his
disciples, Gather up the fragments that remain,
that nothing be lost.

John 6:11–12 (KJV)

To You, from whom everything is received and from
whom nothing is lost, I give myself up this day.
Teach me that all I have is due only to Your
generosity and, even if all I have seems to me small
and insignificant, I know I must still give thanks and
share it with others. Only where Your gifts are freely
shared will I come to see divine abundance. May this
vision create within me a generous heart. But, if
abundance comes, let me not think I am relieved of
giving and sharing, for even then there must be no
waste. Jesus taught us that everything is to be
gathered up and shared again and again. Nothing
must be lost and, in Your love, I know nothing is. So
today, let me act, not as an economist of a worldly
city, but an economist of Your divine kingdom.
Amen.

DAY 21 — GATHERING UP

Evening

O give thanks unto the LORD, for he is good: for his mercy endureth for ever. Let the redeemed of the LORD say so, whom he hath redeemed from the hand of the enemy; And gathered them out of the lands, from the east, and from the west, from the north, and from the south.

Psalm 107:1–3 (KJV)

Eternal God, as Jesus gathered up the fragments of bread and fishes, may I know tonight that You, too, will gather up my soul and protect me from all that threatens. Even when I feel myself separated from You, the story of my faith shows me that You will draw me into Your embrace. May this knowledge that I belong to a gathered people, even when I find myself seemingly alone, help me rest peacefully tonight. I give thanks unto the Lord, for he is good; for his mercy endureth forever. Amen.

DAY 22 — LOST AND FOUND

Morning

I have gone astray like a lost sheep. Seek thy
servant, for I do not forget thy commandments.

Psalm 119:176 (KJV)

O God, I often feel lost, separated from those I love
and from You. I do not know where to turn for help.
If I flee to others, I am often disappointed. If I seek
ways to escape, I always return to myself. As I begin
another day, help me to watch for Your presence
even in the smallest sign; teach me to listen for Your
voice from the least likely person; help me look for
You in the midst of the ordinary. Seek me out, O
Lord, and lead me back to You. Amen.

DAY 22 — LOST AND FOUND

Evening

Jesus said: What man of you, having a hundred sheep, if he lose one of them, doth not leave the ninety and nine and in the wilderness, and go after that which is lost, until he find it?

Luke 15:4 (KJV)

What woman having ten pieces of silver, if she lose one piece, doth not light a candle, and sweep the home, and seek diligently until she find it?

Luke 15:8 (KJV)

For the Son of man is come to seek and to save that which was lost.

Luke 19:10 (KJV)

I will accept Your promise, God, to seek me out, even when I grow weary of ever finding You. In my fear and loneliness, You are preparing a place for me in the presence of my doubts. Though not knowing the way, You are opening a door to me if I would only wait and watch. Now, O Lord, find me willing to accept Your desire for me, waiting for Your light to guide me through the night into the breaking of a new day. In the name of Jesus, who came to save the lost, I pray. Amen.

DAY 23 — BREAKING, GIVING, BLESSING

Morning

And being in Bethany in the house of Simon the leper, as [Jesus] sat at meat, there came a woman having an alabaster box of ointment of spikenard very precious; and she brake the box, and poured it on his head. And there were some that had indignation within themselves, and said, Why was this waste of the ointment made?

Mark 14:3–4 (KJV)

Mysterious God, whose ways so often puzzle me, teach me today how to break open the many alabaster boxes of religious habit that fill my life and so release the precious healing ointments of love and service they contain. May I, like Mary, have the courage to see that the true value of things is not in saving them for some imagined future but in using them as real and immediate needs present themselves to me. Teach me that I can be a healing ointment to the world and that I am here among Your people to be used now. In breaking myself open in Your service I know that my life will never be wasted. Amen.

DAY 23 — BREAKING, GIVING, BLESSING

Evening

Behold, how good and how pleasant it is for [brethren] to dwell together in unity! It is like the precious ointment upon the head, that ran down upon the beard, even Aaron's beard: that went down to the skirts of his garments; As the dew of Hermon, and as the dew that descended upon the mountains of Zion: for there the LORD commanded the blessing, even life for evermore.

Psalm 133 (KJV)

One God of our one world, I come now into Your unifying presence which is like a precious ointment upon the world. May I rest secure in the knowledge that whatever divisions and fractures I have known this day, whether in my own soul or in my relationships with others, all is renewed and restored to wholeness in You. In giving Yourself up to be broken upon the many crosses of this world, Your tears of love and forgiveness have fallen upon me like dew and blessed me with new life and hope. Amen.

DAY 24 — UNIVERSAL SALVATION

Morning

Jesus said: Many shall come from the east and the west, and shall sit down with Abraham, and Isaac, and Jacob, in the kingdom of heaven.

Matthew 8:11 (KJV)

For whosoever shall do the will of my Father, which is in heaven, the same is my brother, and sister, and mother.

Matthew 12:50 (KJV)

God of all people, whose will it is that everyone be saved, I pray this morning that Your kingdom come on earth, as it is in heaven. As I begin another day, help me to remember that others of different cultures and languages and times also seek You, and in seeking have found. Help me to see that people come to You by whatever light they have been given. Let me not judge others without being judged myself. Focus my mind on trusting Your plan that in good time, You will welcome all to Your table for a homecoming feast. Your will be done, God. Amen.

DAY 24 — UNIVERSAL SALVATION

Evening

All the ends of the world shall remember and turn unto the LORD, and all the kindreds of the nations shall worship before thee.

Psalm 22:27 (KJV)

As the evening fades into sleep, God, keep me mindful of the beauty of the world You have made, its diversity and its yet deeper unity, grounded in Your love. Let me not make of my country a national idol, believing only my nation is favoured by You. Let me not make of my religion an object of worship, but only You. Keep fresh before me that it is Your will that not a single person be lost forever and that one day we shall all be one. Amen.

DAY 25 — WONDER

Morning

And [the Shepherds] came with haste, and
found Mary, and Joseph, and the babe lying in
a manger. And when they had seen it, they
made known abroad the saying which was told
them concerning this child. And all they that
heard it wondered at those things which were
told them by the shepherds. But Mary kept all
these things, and pondered them in her heart.

Luke 2:16–19 (KJV)

God of all creation, may I, like the Shepherds, be so
filled with the Wonder of Your presence in this world
that my daily work, though important, does not keep
me from taking time to stop and look at the miracle
of life. Give me the courage to say "No!", just now
and then, to the many demands made upon me so
that I have time go to a place of peace and new
beginnings. Teach me, after these moments of
Wonder, not to rush back to my daily round, but to
wait, like Mary, pondering them and letting them
take root in my heart. Amen.

DAY 25 — WONDER

Evening

I will praise thee; for I am fearfully and wonderfully made: marvellous are thy works; and that my soul knoweth right well.

Psalm 139:14 (KJV)

Creator God, teach me in this time of rest and reflection to consider the miracle of myself, fearfully and wonderfully made. May Your free gift of life cause me to love more deeply and serve more carefully my family, friends and the world. I acknowledge now the Wonder of this universe filled to overflowing with Your marvellous works; my soul knoweth these things right well. Amen.

DAY 26 — REST FOR YOUR SOUL

Morning

Jesus said: Come unto me, all ye that labour and are heavy laden, and I will give you rest. Take my yoke upon you, and learn of me; for I am meek and lowly in heart and you shall find rest unto your souls.

Matthew 11:28–29 (KJV)

As I begin another day, Lord, slow me down, make me mindful of one thing required of me: care of my soul. Days lead unto days and months unto months, and I swim in busyness so that I feel burdened with the cares of the world. Let me keep still, listening for Your voice; let me sit down long enough to hear my name spoken, so that I am not afraid. May the day ahead also refresh my spirit and renew Your calming presence in the midst of life, so that I may be made whole. Have mercy upon me, O Christ, that my soul may find rest in You. Amen.

Evening

Bless the LORD, O my soul, and all that is within me, bless his holy name. Bless the LORD, O my soul, and forget not all his benefits, who hath forgiven all thy iniquities, who healeth all thy diseases, who redeemeth thy life from destruction, who crowneth thee with lovingingkindness and tender mercies, who satisfieth thy mouth with good things so that thy youth is renewed like the eagle's.

Psalm 103:1–5 (KJV)

God, I remember all Your benefits and tender mercies, and as I lie down to rest, I ask that it be a rest in You as well, so that my body and my mind and spirit may be refreshed. Just as day follows night, let a calm repose follow me deep within my heart as I sleep in Your care, trusting that You will not forsake nor leave me. In that knowledge is my strength and respite. Amen.

Morning

Return, we beseech thee, O God of hosts: look down from heaven, and behold, and visit this vine; And the vineyard which thy right hand hath planted, and the branch that thou madest strong for thyself.

Psalm 80:14–15 (KJV)

Today, even when I cannot sense Your presence, I will remember that Your care for the vineyard of the world means You will never abandon it. So, in faith and hope, I will continue to care for all that grows within its walls today and everyday. May I trust and love enough to plant seeds whose strong branches will bear fruit I will never see nor taste. In this hopeful service may my life and work bear witness to the truth that we are but parts of the vine — the holy community which You planted before the dawn of time, whose roots eternally draw nourishment from Your divine, universal wisdom. Amen.

Evening

And [the prodigal son] arose, and came to his father. But when he was yet a great way off, his father saw him, and had compassion, and ran, and fell on his neck, and kissed him.

Luke 15:20 (KJV)

Loving Father, as the time of rest and sleep comes once again, I know that that I can only return to You, for I am Your child. I know that Your love for me means that even when I am still a great way off, You will come out to meet me on the road and guide me safely home. Give me the courage of the prodigal son that, tonight, I may turn towards You and take another small step home. Amen.

DAY 28 — THE HIDDEN GOD

Morning

Now from the sixth hour there was darkness over the land unto the ninth hour. And about the ninth hour Jesus cried with a loud voice, saying: Eli, Eli, lama sabachthani? That is to say, My God, My God, why hast thou forsaken me?

Matthew 27:45–46 (KJV)

There are times, God, when I do not feel Your presence, when You seem to have left me and hidden in the darkness where I cannot find You. I cry out to You, but I hear no response. I need Your help in my present moment, but nothing seems to happen. I grow weary and to the outside world, indifferent. Life seems without hope, and I face the day feeling alone. Though You seem distant and unconcerned, I nonetheless pray today for the strength to wait patiently, to be watchful, not to lose faith. Amen.

DAY 28 — THE HIDDEN GOD

Evening

But unto thee have I cried, O LORD; and in the morning shall my prayer prevent thee? LORD, why castest thou off my soul? Why hidest thou thy face from me?

Psalm 88:13–14 (KJV)

God, I would not feel Your absence so deeply had I not felt Your presence before in the depths of my soul. Even my cries of help are signs that, while You now seem absent, in times before I have known You as a child knows her parent. I cast my life now upon Your mercy and steadfast lovingkindness. Do not hide Your face from me tomorrow; do not cast me off. If my life or prayers have seemed inadequate, forgive me for my shortcomings, and turn me round that I may feel Your presence. Nothing hidden will not be revealed, O Lord, to those who love You. With that understanding, I am made ready for a new day. So be it.

Morning

And [Jesus] said also to the people, "When ye see a cloud rise out of the west, straightway ye say, There cometh a shower; and so it is. And when ye see the south wind blow, ye say, There will be heat; and it cometh to pass. Ye hypocrites, ye can discern the face of the sky and of the earth; but how is it that ye do not discern this time? Yea, and why even of yourselves judge ye not what is right?"

Luke 12:54–57 (KJV)

The spirit of man is the candle of the LORD.

Proverbs 20:27 (KJV)

Lord, teach me today to read and hear Your words wisely — to judge with my fellows, as Jesus taught, what they mean and what is right. Remind me that my own human spirit is Your gift of light, helping me to read Your Word written in my heart; You have enabled me to discern right from wrong, and I need not bow to mere convention. In this task, let me not commit the sin of staying on the surface of Your Word but instead to draw out of it ever new depths of meaning. Your Word is to me, not an instruction manual filled with numbered easy steps to salvation, but the complex story of my people's response to You. So today, above all else, grant me freedom and courage to respond directly to You, without mediator or veil, as did my teacher, the Rabbi Jesus. Amen.

DAY 29 — DISCERNING THE WORD

Evening

In the beginning was the Word, and the Word was with God, and the Word was God.

John 1:1 (KJV)

Let my cry come near before thee, O LORD: give me understanding according to thy word.

Psalm 119:169 (KJV)

By the word of the LORD were the heavens made; and all the host of them by the breath of his mouth.

Psalm 33:6 (KJV)

In the beginning was the Word; in the end, too, Your Word will be. I bring myself now to rest in its eternally creative presence. During the day I have read Your Word with my reason, and have traced it with my fingers as I went about my daily work. Now, in prayer and in reflection, I seek it with my heart. As my eyes can see the glorious Word that is the starry heavens above, may I also come to see Your Word within so that my whole being comes to sing Your praises. Amen.

Morning

I do set my bow in the cloud, and it shall be for a token of a covenant between me and the earth. And it shall come to pass, when I bring a cloud over the earth, that the bow shall be seen in the cloud: And I will remember my covenant, which is between me and you and every living creature of all flesh; and the waters shall no more become a flood to destroy all flesh.

Genesis 9:13–15 (KJV)

Loving God, when I see or hear of terrible events in this world, may my glimpses of Your kingdom seen in better times and prayer, sustain me. At times it will seem to some that You have brought these disasters upon humankind; faith and hope in You will seem unreasonable and unfounded. Yet recall me to the knowledge that Your Love is infinite and that I must not judge You or Your world by my own standards. Remind me that the rainbow of Your loving and forgiving Covenant remains ever present. So help me to grieve with my brothers and sisters and then direct my head, heart and hands in imitation of Your Divine Love revealed to us in Jesus. In this Divine Love, alone, I trust. Amen.

Evening

[Jesus prayed] That they all may be one; as thou, Father, art in me, and I in thee, that they also may be one in us: that the world may believe that thou hast sent me. And the glory which thou gavest me I have given them; that they may be one, even as we are one: I in them, and thou in me, that they may be made perfect in one; and that the world may know that thou hast sent me, and hast loved them, as thou hast loved me.

John 17:21–23 (KJV)

Then the soldiers, when they had crucified Jesus, took his garments, and made four parts, to every soldier a part; and also his coat: now the coat was without seam, woven from the top throughout.

John 19:23 (KJV)

One God of our one world, I come once more into Your unifying presence. Remind me that my own and all life is intimately woven into the very fabric of being — a seamless garment that cannot be torn apart. Tonight, teach me to understand, as did my forbears, that beneath the apparent diversities and divisions of this world there is an interdependent unity of all things. May I sleep soundly in the knowledge of this unity so that, tomorrow, I wake refreshed and able to witness to it in my thoughts, words and deeds. Amen.

DAY 31 — THE STONE ROLLED AWAY

Morning

The LORD is my light and my salvation; whom shall I fear? the LORD is the strength of my life; of whom shall I be afraid? Wait on the LORD: be of good courage, and he shall strengthen thine heart: wait I say on the LORD.

Psalm 27:1, 14 (KJV)

Be of good cheer, O my soul, the Lord is the light of my light, the source of my strength, the promise of my future. I have waited on You, God, and You have strengthened my heart and restored my zest for life. You have not hidden Your face from me forever, but planted deep within me a spirit of hope and joy and lovingkindness that will never leave me, in this life or the next. My strength is renewed and my soul sings praises to Your name. I begin this day anew, knowing that even when I cannot feel You, You remain with me, deep within and without, in the presence of friends and family and strangers; in nature and the heavens; in the law You have planted in every open heart. Amen.

DAY 31 — THE STONE ROLLED AWAY

Evening

And [Joseph of Arimathaea] bought fine linen, and took [Jesus] down, and wrapped him in the linen, and laid him in a sepulchre which was hewn out of a rock, and rolled a stone unto the door of the sepulchre.

Mark 15:46 (KJV)

And when the sabbath was past, Mary Magdalene, and Mary the mother of James, and Salome, had brought sweet spices that they might come and anoint [Jesus]....And they said unto themselves, Who shall roll away the stone from the door of the sepulchre? And when they looked, they saw that the stone was rolled away....And entering into the sepulchre, they saw a young man sitting on the right side....And he saith unto them, Be not affrighted. Ye seek Jesus of Nazareth, which was crucified. He is risen. He is not here. Behold the place where they laid him.

Mark 16:1, 3–6 (KJV)

O Lord, roll the stone away from my eyes that I may behold Your glory and Your victory over death itself. For what was hidden has now been revealed, what was lost, found. From this time hence, let me walk with courage and hope, knowing that love is stronger than death. In the name of Jesus, my brother and liberator. Amen.

A PLAN FOR INDIVIDUAL RETREATS

It is often assumed that if you want to experience a retreat, you must travel somewhere to be with a group led by a trained facilitator. Neither of these assumptions need be true. You can stay put, pray by yourself, and be solitary.

Jesus began his own ministry only after spending time alone in the wilderness where he began the process of discerning what his life's work would be (Matthew 4:1ff; Mark 1:12ff; Luke 4:1ff). Shortly afterwards, having called his disciples and begun to heal the sick, Jesus prepared to begin preaching in Galilee in the same way:

> And in the morning, rising up a great while before day, he went out, and departed into a solitary place, and there prayed (Mark 1:35).

Matthew (6:6) also reports Jesus saying:

> But thou, when thou prayest, enter into thy closet, and when thou has shut thy door, pray to thy Father which is in secret; and thy Father which seeth in secret shall reward thee openly.

It is important to follow this example of Jesus by taking time every day, whether in the morning or the evening, to be alone with God. When Matthew reports Jesus saying that you need to find a place to pray, a 'closet,' he means a place where you can shut the door and be alone. For some people, nothing more is needed than a space. Others may choose to build an 'altar' and place on it candles or flowers or other reminders of their faith. Some choose to stand while others sit. Some bring Bibles or other devotional books; others, no books. Some fold their hands in prayers, use prayer beads or ropes; others do none of these things. The purpose of this time is simply to relate to God, not to find the right words or gestures or scriptures. Some find it helpful to stay in silence; others find a word or phrase to repeat quietly over and over, such as 'Christ have mercy on me,' 'shalom' or the ancient Christian 'maranatha' prayer (meaning 'our Lord come'). Some people give thanks for what they have. Some pray for themselves or others who are facing life issues. Some remember those they love who are gone and others ask for God's mercy. Some confess their shortcomings; others ask for forgiveness. The most important thing is taking time to be alone with yourself and God.

PART THREE
COMMUNAL WORSHIP

FROM PRIVATE TO COMMUNAL WORSHIP
Moving from Individuals to Groups
The Process of Small Group Ministries

The Book of Acts records this about the early Christian communities:

> And they continued steadfastly in the apostles' doctrine and fellowship, and in breaking of bread, and in prayers (Acts 2:42).

The earliest pattern, therefore, was to foster discipleship within the context of small groups where people could come to know one another and grow together. The basic purposes of these small groups included learning the basic tenets of their faith, study of scripture, worship, eating together, fellowship, supporting one another's ministries as disciples of Jesus, and serving others. Communion was observed regularly as a way to remember Jesus and to help live out his commandments.

These small groups or cells often arose out of larger communities (e.g., temples or synagogues), but met in one another's homes, usually on a weekly basis, and certainly in small groups, probably no more than twelve persons.

It is interesting to note that some of the most reforming times in the later Christian movement grew out of these small groups or house churches. One of the notable examples is the German Pietist movement which arose from small groups ('conventicles') which later helped to reform the larger congregations and also spread the message not only in Europe but also into the new world of America. This movement continues today in many traditions where small group ministries take place within the context of large congregations, and also within house churches. In fact, not only are house churches one of the fastest growing segments of the British and American religious scene, but some of the largest churches have also adopted the small group process as part of their strategy. The principle here is that churches grow by subtraction (many multiplying cells or groups), not addition (taking members into a single organization one by one).

Each small group adopts its own processes, but often exhibits these elements:

1. Group meets weekly in homes of participants
2. A meal is shared first
3. Individuals share what they wish from their lives, especially as it pertains to their faith journeys
4. Reading and discussion of scripture (assigned beforehand)
5. Prayer
6. Service to others (the group itself or individuals in the group select a hands-on project to serve others).
7. Communion

The purpose of this process is sometimes to create self-sustaining house churches and at others to help renew the larger church body. Whichever purpose is followed, growing in faith requires both individual and group disciplines. A good resource for starting a church at home is *House Church Manual*, William Tenny-Brittain (St. Louis: Missouri: Chalice Press, 2004). Another resource that arose out of private devotion is *Awakening the Soul*, John Morgan (Boston: Skinner House Books, 2001).

READINGS AND PRAYERS FOR THE HOME
At Christmas, Easter and Pentecost

CHRISTMAS EVE

Now the birth of Jesus Christ was on this wise: When as his mother Mary was espoused to Joseph, before they came together, she was found with child of the Holy Ghost. Then Joseph her husband, being a just man, and not willing to make her a publick example, was minded to put her away privily. But while he thought on these things, behold, the angel of the Lord appeared unto him in a dream, saying, Joseph, thou son of David, fear not to take unto thee Mary thy wife: for that which is conceived in her is of the Holy Ghost. And she shall bring forth a son, and thou shalt call his name JESUS: for he shall save his people from their sins. Now all this was done, that it might be fulfilled which was spoken of the Lord by the prophet, saying, Behold, a virgin shall be with child, and shall bring forth a son, and they shall call his name Emmanuel, which being interpreted is, God with us. Then Joseph being raised from sleep did as the angel of the Lord had bidden him, and took unto him his wife: And knew her not till she had brought forth her firstborn son: and he called his name JESUS.

Matthew 1:18–25 (KJV)

Eternal God, we gather together this Christmas Eve to remember the evening when a Divine Light was born into our world — Emmanuel, God with us, Jesus of Nazareth. This birth did not come with all the pomp and circumstance which surrounds the coming of earthly power but simply, in a stable. In this, our ancient and beloved story, we are reminded always to be expectant and that no place is so ordinary or so poor that the Divine cannot be born there. So may this, our ordinary home, be a time and place when the Divine Light is once again brought to birth in our own hearts. May we be so filled with Your presence that all the days which follow will be filled with a new and ever-growing Spirit. Amen.

CHRISTMAS DAY

And it came to pass in those days, that there went out a decree from Caesar Augustus, that all the world should be taxed. (And this taxing was first made when Cyrenius was governor of Syria.) And all went to be taxed, every one into his own city. And Joseph also went up from Galilee, out of the city of Nazareth, into Judaea, unto the city of David, which is called Bethlehem; (because he was of the house and lineage of David:) To be taxed with Mary his espoused wife, being great with child. And so it was, that, while they were there, the days were accomplished that she should be delivered. And she brought forth her firstborn son, and wrapped him in swaddling clothes, and laid him in a manger; because there was no room for them in the inn. And there were in the same country shepherds abiding in the field, keeping watch over their flock by night. And, lo, the angel of the Lord came upon them, and the glory of the Lord shone round about them: and they were sore afraid. And the angel said unto them, Fear not: for, behold, I bring you good tidings of great joy, which shall be to all people. For unto you is born this day in the city of David a Saviour, which is Christ the Lord. And this shall be a sign unto you; Ye shall find the babe wrapped in swaddling clothes, lying in a manger. And suddenly there was with the angel a multitude of the heavenly host praising God, and saying, Glory to God in the highest, and on earth peace, good will toward men. And it came to pass, as the angels were gone away from them into heaven, the shepherds said one to another, Let us now go even unto Bethlehem, and see this thing which is come to pass, which the Lord hath made known unto us. And they came with haste, and found Mary, and Joseph, and the babe lying in a manger. And when they had seen it, they made known abroad the saying which was told them concerning this child. And all they that heard it wondered at those things which were told them by the shepherds. But Mary kept all these things, and pondered them in her heart. And the shepherds returned, glorifying and praising God for all the things that they had heard and seen, as it was told unto them

Luke 2:1–20 (KJV)

God of new beginnings, let this be a day of thanks and wonder for us. May the birth of Jesus which we celebrate today find its echo in all our actions. Remind us, too, of the wisdom of the mystic who knew that Christ could be born a thousand times in Bethlehem but that if he were not born again in each of us, all would be in vain. So help us make this and all homes the crib-side. Help us become angels,

shepherds and kings and, above all else, teach us to
be parents of Your divinity in this our world.

GOOD FRIDAY

And as they led him away, they laid hold upon
one Simon, a Cyrenian, coming out of the
country, and on him they laid the cross, that he
might bear it after Jesus. And there followed
him a great company of people, and of
women, which also bewailed and lamented
him. But Jesus turning unto them said,
Daughters of Jerusalem, weep not for me, but
weep for yourselves, and for your children. For,
behold, the days are coming, in the which they
shall say, Blessed are the barren, and the
wombs that never bare, and the paps which
never gave suck. Then shall they begin to say
to the mountains, Fall on us; and to the hills,
Cover us. For if they do these things in a green
tree, what shall be done in the dry? And there
were also two other, malefactors, led with him
to be put to death. And when they were come
to the place, which is called Calvary, there they
crucified him, and the malefactors, one on the
right hand, and the other on the left. Then said
Jesus, Father, forgive them; for they know not
what they do. And they parted his raiment, and
cast lots. And the people stood beholding. And
the rulers also with them derided [him], saying,
He saved others; let him save himself, if he be
Christ, the chosen of God. And the soldiers also
mocked him, coming to him, and offering him

vinegar, And saying, If thou be the king of the Jews, save thyself. And a superscription also was written over him in letters of Greek, and Latin, and Hebrew, THIS IS THE KING OF THE JEWS. And one of the malefactors which were hanged railed on him, saying, If thou be Christ, save thyself and us. But the other answering rebuked him, saying, Dost not thou fear God, seeing thou art in the same condemnation? And we indeed justly; for we receive the due reward of our deeds: but this man hath done nothing amiss. And he said unto Jesus, Lord, remember me when thou comest into thy kingdom. And Jesus said unto him, Verily I say unto thee, To day shalt thou be with me in paradise. And it was about the sixth hour, and there was a darkness over all the earth until the ninth hour. And the sun was darkened, and the veil of the temple was rent in the midst. And when Jesus had cried with a loud voice, he said, Father, into thy hands I commend my spirit: and having said thus, he gave up the ghost. Now when the centurion saw what was done, he glorified God, saying, Certainly this was a righteous man. And all the people that came together to that sight, beholding the things which were done, smote their breasts, and returned. And all his acquaintance, and the women that followed him from Galilee, stood afar off, beholding these things.

Luke 23:26–49 (KJV)

Loving God, be with us today as we remember the sacrifice made for us by Your faithful servant Jesus, Your son and our brother. Teach us the lessons of this dreadful time: that moments which seem utterly barren can ultimately bring forth new life; that we must forgive those who act in ignorance of Your saving love; that we can be so confident in Your love that we can commit our spirits to You. Teach us that nothing of true worth and value is ever lost, no matter how it looks from the foot of the cross. Teach us, too, that Your spirit is a seamless garment which can never truly be divided. May the knowledge of Easter Sunday's promise help us through our dark days of despair to remain for ever servants of Your kingdom of love, justice and mercy. Amen.

HOLY SATURDAY

And, behold, there was a man named Joseph, a counsellor; and he was a good man, and a just: (The same had not consented to the counsel and deed of them;) he was of Arimathaea, a city of the Jews: who also himself waited for the kingdom of God. This man went unto Pilate, and begged the body of Jesus. And he took it down, and wrapped it in linen, and laid it in a sepulchre that was hewn in stone, wherein never man before was laid. And that day was the preparation, and the sabbath drew on. And the women also, which came with him from Galilee, followed after, and beheld the sepulchre, and how his body was laid. And they returned, and prepared spices and ointments; and rested the sabbath day according to the commandment

Luke 23:50–56 (KJV)

God of Infinite Hope, after the shock of all our losses, and before the experience of a new and full life has entered our hearts, help us to live honourably and blameless in the dark and empty days of our lives. Help us to continue to serve You well, decently and in good order, even though it seems the very foundations of our lives have crumbled and we have come to believe that we built on sand. Teach us, on this saddest of days, the chief lesson of grief and loss, that we must wait patiently for You to return life and hope to our souls. Help us acknowledge that there is no speedy nor easy path that we can travel in these times, and that in love and hope we must simply wait, grieve, rest and pray. Amen.

EASTER SUNDAY

And, behold, two of [the disciples] went that same day to a village called Emmaus, which was from Jerusalem about threescore furlongs. they talked together of all these things which had happened. And it came to pass, that, while they communed together and reasoned, Jesus himself drew near, and went with them. But their eyes were holden that they should not know him. And he said unto them, What manner of communications are these that ye have one to another, as ye walk, and are sad? And the one of them, whose name was Cleopas, answering said unto him, Art thou only a stranger in Jerusalem, and hast not known the things which are come to pass there in these days? And he said unto them, What things? And they said unto him, Concerning Jesus of Nazareth, which was a prophet mighty in deed and word before God and all the people: And how the chief priests and our rulers delivered him to be condemned to death, and have crucified him. But we trusted that it had been he which should have redeemed Israel: and beside all this, to day is the third day since these things were done. Yea, and certain women also of our company made us astonished, which were early at the sepulchre; And when they found not his body, they came, saying, that they had also seen a vision of angels, which said that he was alive. And certain of them which were with us went to the sepulchre, and found it even so as the women had said: but him they saw not. Then he said unto them, O fools, and slow of heart to believe all that the prophets have spoken: Ought not Christ to have suffered these things, and to enter into his glory? And beginning at Moses and all the prophets, he expounded unto them in all the scriptures the things concerning himself. And they drew nigh unto the village, whither they went: and he made as though he would have gone further. But they constrained him, saying, Abide with us: for it is toward evening, and the day is far spent. And he went in to tarry with them. And it came to pass, as he sat at meat with them, he took bread, and blessed it, and brake, and gave to them. And their eyes were opened, and they knew him; and he vanished out of their sight. And they said one to another, Did not our heart burn within us, while he talked with us by the way, and while he opened to us the scriptures? And they rose up the same hour, and returned to Jerusalem, and found the eleven gathered together, and them that were with them, Saying, The Lord is risen indeed, and hath appeared to Simon. And they told what things were done in the way, and how he was known of them in breaking of bread

Luke 24:13–35 (KJV)

Sustaining God, we are reminded that the dark days only pass slowly from our saddened hearts and that we walk side-by-side with reborn hope for many miles before we can recognize its presence. Then, in simple human acts, the shared journey, the familiar voice, the breaking of bread in community, we suddenly encounter the centre of creation face to face. All loss is restored, all grief turned to joy, all death to life. May this Easter Day and its joy remain in our hearts always as a light in the darkness which is never overcome. Amen.

PENTECOST

And when the day of Pentecost was fully come, they were all with one accord in one place. And suddenly there came a sound from heaven as of a rushing mighty wind, and it filled all the house where they were sitting. And there appeared unto them cloven tongues like as of fire, and it sat upon each of them. And they were all filled with the Holy Ghost, and began to speak with other tongues, as the Spirit gave them utterance. And there were dwelling at Jerusalem Jews, devout men, out of every nation under heaven. Now when this was noised abroad, the multitude came together, and were confounded, because that every man heard them speak in his own language. And they were all amazed and marvelled, saying one to another, Behold, are not all these which speak Galilaeans? And how hear we every man in our own tongue, wherein we were born? Parthians, and Medes, and Elamites, and the dwellers in Mesopotamia, and in Judaea, and Cappadocia, in Pontus, and Asia, Phrygia, and Pamphylia, in Egypt, and in the parts of Libya about Cyrene, and strangers of Rome, Jews and proselytes, Cretes and Arabians, we do hear them speak in our tongues the wonderful works of God. And they were all amazed, and were in doubt, saying one to another, What meaneth this? Others mocking said, These men are full of new wine. But Peter, standing up with the eleven, lifted up his voice, and said unto them, Ye men of Judaea, and all ye that dwell at Jerusalem, be this known unto you, and hearken to my words: For these are not drunken, as ye suppose, seeing it is but the third hour of the day. But this is that which was spoken by the prophet Joel; And it shall come to pass in the last days, saith God, I will pour out of my Spirit upon all flesh: and your sons and your daughters shall prophesy, and your young men shall see visions, and your old men shall dream dreams: And on my servants and on my handmaidens I will pour out in those days of my Spirit; and they shall prophesy: And I will shew wonders in heaven above, and signs in the earth beneath; blood, and fire, and vapour of smoke: The sun shall be turned into darkness, and the moon into blood, before that great and notable day of the Lord come: And it shall come to pass, that whosoever shall call on the name of the Lord shall be saved.

Acts 2:1–21 (KJV)

God of eternal and universal inspiration, we give thanks today for Your promise that You will pour out Your spirit upon all people. May we have wisdom to know that, in the moment we mark the founding of our Christian community of faith, we do not also mark the end of Your work amongst us. From the beginning of time to this hour, Your spirit continues to inspire young and old, Christian and Jew, Muslim and Buddhist, Hindu and Jain. May we keep alive to the many voices of Your holy spirit and always celebrate the life giving flame of Your presence among all humankind. Amen.

THREE COMMUNION SERVICES

The communion service is one of the deepest and most vital parts for many communities called by Jesus. It serves to help us remember his life, teachings, death, and resurrection. The communion services below may be used before or after any gathering or by themselves.

FIRST COMMUNION SERVICE

Our seventeenth century Polish Socinian forbears taught the oneness of God and the humanity of Jesus. While the communion service below may not be one of theirs, the closing prayer is, as are the themes of companionship and shared ministry. In this communion, people gather in a circle or in small groups of no more than six people. Bread and water/wine are the elements used and people serve the communion to one another.

¶ *Each person in turn administers communion to their neighbour saying:*

> I give you this bread of life, dear friend, that you may be nourished in mind and body (*give bread*).

> I give you this water/wine of life, dear friend, that you may be strengthened (*give water/wine*).

> I give you this time, dear friend, that you may tell me who you are (*people may respond in a few words*).

> I give you this sign of respect, dear friend, that you may understand that while we are different, we travel the same road (*give the right hand of fellowship or, if appropriate, the kiss of peace on the forehead*).

¶ *Say together the closing prayer:*

Gather or scatter us, O Lord, according to Your will. Build us into one Church, a Church with open doors and large windows, a Church which takes this world seriously, ready to work and to suffer, and even to bleed for it. Amen.

SECOND COMMUNION SERVICE

Service-leader: We begin by joining together in a time of silence, bringing ourselves to rest in the presence of God.

¶ *Silence*

Service-leader: Let us now join together in saying the prayer Jesus taught all those beginning in the life of the Spirit, the Lord's Prayer:

> Our Father, who art in heaven, hallowed be thy name. Thy kingdom come. Thy will be done on earth, as it is in heaven. Give us this day our daily bread. And forgive us our trespasses, as we forgive those who trespass against us. And lead us not into temptation; but deliver us from evil. For thine is the kingdom, the power and the glory, for ever and ever. Amen.

Service-leader: Remembering we have been taught that 'if we confess our sins, God who is faithful and just will forgive us our sins and cleanse us from all unrighteousness' (1 John 1:9), let us now join together in saying this prayer of confession:

> O God, we acknowledge that we have often failed to keep the peace in our midst and have hurt others and ourselves by thought, word and deed. In silence now, we confess our failings.

¶ *Silence*

Service-leader: The Lord Jesus on the night when he was betrayed took a loaf of bread, and when he had given thanks, he broke it and said, "This is my body that is for you. Do this in remembrance of me." In the same way he took the cup also, after supper, saying, "This cup is the new covenant in my blood. Do this, as often as you drink it, in remembrance of me."

1 Corinthians 11:23–25 (NRSV)

With what shall I come before the LORD, and bow myself before God on high? He has told you, O mortal, what is good; and what does the LORD require of you but to do justice, and to love kindness, and to walk humbly with your God?

Micah 6:6, 8 (NRSV)

Eternal and Loving God, we give thanks that You have let us walk in the footsteps of so many good and faithful men and women. In this service, we remember all who have acted in accord with Your Word, wisdom and love and have walked humbly with You; all whose lives have been beautiful with the same divine beauty revealed to us in Jesus. Let this cloud of witnesses be to us an example of godly life, and by faith, hope and love may we be united with them and You. Amen.

¶ *Lifting the unbroken bread, the service-leader breaks it and says:*

Service-leader: As all share in the bread of life and are children of God, we break this bread as a sign and symbol of Jesus, of all who have faithfully served God and humankind, and as a reminder of our desire to serve one another in perfect love.

¶ *The bread is now shared in silence with each person in turn offering it to their neighbour.*

¶ *Lifting the cup, the service-leader says:*

Service-leader: As we are all made of one blood and together share this world, we take this cup as a sign and symbol of Jesus, of all who have witnessed to the unity of humankind, and as a reminder of our desire, that freely as we have received, freely we will give.

¶ *The wine is now shared in silence with each person in turn offering it to their neighbour.*

¶ *Silence*

Service-leader: Hear, O Israel: the Lord our God, the Lord is one; you shall love the Lord your God with all your heart, and with all your soul, and with all your mind, and with all your strength. And a second is like it: You shall love your neighbour as yourself. There is no other commandment greater than these. On these two commandments hang all the law and the prophets. If you know these things, you are blessed if you do them.

Mark 12:29–31; Matthew 22:40; John 13:17 (NRSV)

Let us go in peace. Amen.

THIRD COMMUNION SERVICE

¶ *Say together the following invocation and covenant:*

We come into Your presence, God, as disciples of Jesus who called us to be his brothers and sisters. Plant deep within our hearts his spirit that we may know his love surrounds us here.

Love is the doctrine of this church, the quest of truth its sacrament, and service is its prayer. To dwell together in peace, to seek knowledge in freedom, to serve humanity in fellowship, to the end that all souls shall grow into harmony with the Divine — thus do we covenant with each other and with God.

Revd L. Griswold Williams

¶ *Here may follow a hymn or some music and the Lord's Prayer may be said.*

Service-leader: Let us join in confessing our sins before God:

O God, we come into Your presence, not trusting in our own righteousness, but in Your manifold and abiding mercies. We are ashamed of our selfish ways. Here we would be turned to the way of Jesus' brave and tender spirit, and find that wholeness of life which shall be at once a divine blessing for us and a divine mystery. Forgive our failures and shortcomings, and by Your grace strengthen our weak desires for goodness, that we may henceforth serve You without fear or shame.

Service-leader: Be assured that as we confess our sins and pledge to change our ways, we are forgiven.

¶ *Reading:*

And they drew nigh unto the village, whither they went: and he made as though he would have gone further. But they constrained him, saying, "Abide with us: for it is toward evening, and the day is far spent." And he went in to tarry with them. And it came to pass, as he sat at meat with them, he took bread, and blessed [it], and brake, and gave to them. And their eyes were opened, and they knew him; and he vanished out of their sight. And they said one to another, "Did not our heart burn within us, while he talked with us by the way, and while he opened to us the scriptures?"

Luke 24:28–32 (KJV)

¶ *Say together the following prayer:*

O God, draw together in one accord the spirits of Your children until each shall labour in their appointed way for the kingdom of love. We ask this in the name of Jesus, our teacher and friend.

Service-leader: By this all shall know that you are my disciples, if you love one another.

John 13:34–35 (KJV)

¶ *Say together the following words:*

Let us partake in spirit with those who, remembering him, have shared the bread of life and the wine of sacrifice. Blessed are they that hunger and thirst after righteousness, for they shall be filled.

¶ *People now serve the bread and wine/water to their neighbour with the following words:*

(In the giving of bread) Take and eat this in remembrance of Jesus.

(In the giving of wine) Take and drink this in remembrance of Jesus.

¶ *Here may follow a hymn or some music*

Service-leader: Go in peace, to love and to serve as Jesus has commanded you. And may God's spirit be with you and with all those you love. Amen.

A CHILD DEDICATION or BAPTISM
An adaptation of a ceremony by Revd Clifford M. Reed

Service Leader: We are gathered here today to welcome and to bless/baptise *(name)* and for *(name)* and/or *(name)* to dedicate themselves to his/her nurture.

In this ceremony we celebrate life's continual renewal and we welcome this child to life's larger community, seeking God's blessing upon him/her. We give thanks for the gift of a son/daughter to *(name)* and *(name)*. In this service, they declare their dedication to his/her loving care. For all of us, it is an opportunity to pledge our support to them as a family.

¶ *The reading:*

At that time the disciples came to Jesus and asked, "Who is the greatest in the kingdom of heaven?" He called a child, whom he put among them, and said, "Truly I tell you, unless you change and become like children, you will never enter the kingdom of heaven. Whoever becomes humble like this child is the greatest in the kingdom of heaven. Whoever welcomes one such child in my name welcomes me."

Matthew 18:1–5 (NRSV)

Service Leader: (*name*) and/or (*name*), in seeking the welcoming and blessing of (*name*) you dedicate yourselves to the fullest development of his/her unique potential. In seeking for him/her the blessing of our free faith and the Universal Church, you pledge to encourage in him/her, to the best of your ability, the love of truth, the vision of peace and the sense of belonging to one human family.

Do you each promise that by your teaching and example, you will help him/her to be reverent and strong, and equal to the tasks and temptations that will confront him/her?

Parents: I do.

¶ *Here the parents may offer additional promises in their own words.*

Service Leader: Your child is the wonderful creation of your lives together. It is your desire to make life for him/her as wonderful as it can be. May this brief ceremony be for you a symbol of your gratitude and your resolution.

Do each of you as godparents promise to support (*name*) and (*name*) in their task of parenthood?

Godparents: I do.

¶ *Here the Godparents may offer additional promises in their own words.*

Service Leader: What name have you given this child?

Parents: (*name*)

Service Leader: (*name*), In the name of God [or, *In the name of God our Father and in the Spirit of his Son, our Brother, Jesus* or, *In the name of the Father, the Son, and the Holy Spirit*] we welcome you to the human family and to the earth, our common home. We welcome you with water, symbol of the purity with which you were born; and with a flower, symbol of the beauty which is yours. May God bless you as we bless you, and may the divine spirit in your heart guide you, comfort you and strengthen you all the days of your life. Amen.

Service Leader: Let us join together in a time of prayer and reflection:

Eternal and loving God, for the gift of childhood whose innocence and laughter keep the world young, we all rejoice and give thanks. May this sweet life, which we have welcomed into our community of ideals and friendship, receive abundantly the blessings of health, love, knowledge and wisdom, and in his/her turn may he/she give back richly to the common heritage that endures from generation to generation. This we ask in the spirit of our brother Jesus and all your messengers. Amen.

A MEETING FOR BIBLE STUDY

It is important for us to gather together to learn about our Christian faith from the record of Holy Scripture. However, we must do this in a way that allows mutual understanding to grow as each of us brings to the common table of study, not only historical knowledge, but also our personal spiritual insights and experiences. The truths of scripture can be drawn out only when we meet, freely and without fear of censure, in open and loving conversation.

¶ *Opening Prayer:*

God of all wisdom, remembering that Jesus called upon us to seek so that we should find, we gather here as honest seekers after Your truth. In our long journey of faith we have discovered that Your truth is to be found, not only in our own Holy Scripture, but also in the Book of Nature and in each human soul. We also acknowledge that Your truth can be found in the writings of the other beautiful faiths which grace our world. Knowing these things, may our search for Truth in our own beloved scripture always be guided, not by sectarian prejudice, but only by the presence of Your universal guiding spirit and law. Amen.

¶ *Bible Reading & Conversation*

Finally, brothers and sisters, whatsoever things are true, whatsoever things are honest, whatsoever things are just, whatsoever things are pure, whatsoever things are lovely, whatsoever things are of good report; if there be any virtue, and if there be any praise, think on these things. These things, which we have learned, received, heard, and seen together we must do: and then the God of peace shall be with us. Amen.

Adapted from Philippians 4:8–9

A SERVICE OF PRIVATE CONFESSION

Sometimes we are called upon by individuals to hear their confession. This private service begins the necessary process of restoring right relationships with ourselves, with others, and with God.

Confessor: Forgiving, just and merciful God, we come before You now to reaffirm our intention to lead the kind of life Jesus taught us to live and, in his spirit, to confess our wrongdoings. May we find here the freedom of forgiveness, not simply to forget our sins, but instead, to make them seeds of a renewed and more fruitful life of worship and service. Above all, we remember Jesus promised us that if we forgive others we, too, shall be forgiven (Luke 6:37). Now let us pray together the prayer he taught all those beginning in the life of the Spirit:

> Our Father, who art in heaven, hallowed be thy name. Thy kingdom come. Thy will be done on earth, as it is in heaven. Give us this day our daily bread. And forgive us our trespasses, as we forgive those who trespass against us. And lead us not into temptation; but deliver us from evil. For thine is the kingdom, the power and the glory, for ever and ever. Amen.

¶ *A short time of silence to be kept*

Confessor: Let us now confess our sins to each other.

¶ *The confession*

Confessor: Having begun by forgiving others and concluded by confessing our own wrongdoings, let us now prepare to leave this place with a sense that a new start is always possible with God, who is love. All He requires from us is to do justly, to love mercy, and to walk humbly with Him. Jesus, knowing this, taught us two great commandments:

> Hear, O Israel; The Lord our God is one Lord: And thou shalt love the Lord thy God with all thy heart, and with all thy soul, and with all thy mind, and with all thy strength: this is the first commandment. And the second is like, namely this, Thou shalt love thy neighbour as thyself. There is none other commandment greater than these.
>
> *Matthew 12:29-31* (KJV)

Let us leave by praying together with the Psalmist:

> Create in us a clean heart, O God; and renew a right spirit within us. Amen.
>
> *Adapted from Psalm 51:10*

PRAYERS FOR CONFESSION AND RECONCILIATION IN GROUP SETTINGS

Often in the life of a group or gathering, people are wounded or hurt by words or deeds of others. Seldom do we take the time to face these hurts and deal with them prayerfully. Yet, unless these feelings are dealt with wounds fester and they return, usually with greater force. The prayers below are intended for such times.

Service Leader: Have mercy, O God, according to thy lovingkindness, according unto the multitude of thy tender mercies blot out our transgressions. Wash us thoroughly from our iniquities, and cleanse us from our sin. For we acknowledge our transgressions and our sin is everywhere before us.

Adapted from Psalm 51:1–3

O God, we acknowledge that we have failed to keep the peace in our midst and that we have hurt others and ourselves by word and deed. In silence now, we confess our sins.

¶ *Silence*

Create in us a clean heart, O God, and renew a right spirit within us.

Adapted from Psalm 51:10

Service Leader: Let us conclude by saying together the Lord's Prayer:

> Our Father, who art in heaven, hallowed be thy name. Thy kingdom come. Thy will be done on earth, as it is in heaven. Give us this day our daily bread. And forgive us our trespasses, as we forgive those who trespass against us. And lead us not into temptation; but deliver us from evil. For thine is the kingdom, the power and the glory, for ever and ever. Amen.

A SERVICE OF REMEMBRANCE (Memorial)

Whether a loss is recent or stretches back in time, we need to remember those we love who are no longer physically present. This simple service can be used by groups or communities who wish, from time to time, to call by name those lost to them. It is important to the bonding of any group that a regular time be given (perhaps at special times of year — autumn, Christmas, Easter, etc.) to remember those who have been lost,

Service Leader: We come together as people of faith knowing that You have promised us that love is stronger than death.

¶ *Light a candle and say:*

We light this candle remembering (*names of those to be remembered*), trusting that the Divine Presence symbolized by the light of this candle is present, even when the flame is extinguished.

¶ *Readings:*

> As for mortals, their days are like grass: they flourish like a flower of the field. But the steadfast love of the LORD is from everlasting to everlasting on those who fear him, and his righteousness to children's children.
>
> *Psalm 103:15; 17 (NRSV)*

> Jesus said: I am the resurrection, and the life: he that believeth in me, though he were dead, yet shall he live: And whosoever liveth and believeth in me shall never die.
>
> *John 11:25–26 (KJV)*

Service Leader: In silence, we gather together now remembering those we have lost.

¶ *Silence*

Out of the silence, we remember them. Anyone who wishes may say a few words.

¶ *Remembrances...*

Service Leader: O God, You have said that we should not be afraid, but often our loss seems more than we can bear. Implant in us a deep sense that the veil which separates life from death is more fragile than we imagine, and that our loved ones are near to us now and wait for us just beyond the corner of our time. We remember. We feel the loss but also trust that You have prepared a homecoming. We pray in the name of Christ, who gave us Life Everlasting. Amen.

WORDS FOR THE SICK

And great multitudes came unto him, having with them those that were lame, blind, dumb, maimed, and many others, and cast them down at Jesus' feet; and he healed them

Matthew 15:30 (KJV)

O God, we come into Your presence knowing our own infirmities, and we are anxious about what the future holds. We rest in Your presence trusting in Your care for us and especially for Your servant (*name*). Not our, but Your will be done. Knowing this, we can accept whatever comes. In Jesus' name we pray. Amen.

WORDS FOR THE LOSS OF A CHILD

And they brought unto him also infants that he would touch them; but when his disciples saw it, they rebuked them. But Jesus called them unto him, and said, "Suffer the little children to come unto me, and forbid them not: for of such is the kingdom of heaven.

Luke 18:15–16 (KJV)

Parent God, who loves and welcomes us home no matter our age, we remember how Jesus called children into his kingdom and said they were close to his heart. We who measure life by days and months and years are stricken with the loss of our child, but trust that she/he is gathered in Your arms again so that one day we shall celebrate a reunion with him/her. We grieve now and rightly so. But one day we shall find one another in that place where death has no power over our spirits. In the name of Jesus who welcomed children into the kingdom of God. Amen.

A SCATTERING OF ASHES OR INTERMENT

Jesus said: The wind bloweth where it listeth, and thou hearest the sound thereof, but canst not tell whence it cometh, and whither it goeth: so is every one that is born of the Spirit

John 3:8 (KJV)

Eternal God, though we can never know fully what follows the moment of death, we remain assured that Your loving spirit dwells in us and upholds and sustains all creation. So, in confidence, we now release/commit (*name*) body to the air/ground as a sign and symbol of the Spirit's return home to Your Kingdom. Amen.

PRAYERS OF THANKSGIVING

These prayers of thanksgiving may be used by small gatherings around mealtime, before a special meeting, with children, etc.

It is a good thing to give thanks unto the LORD, and to sing praises unto thy name, O most High; to shew forth thy lovingkindness in the morning and thy faithfulness every night. For thou, LORD, hast made me glad though thy work.

Psalm 92:1–3, 5 (KJV)

Let us gather together in common prayer, understanding that what unites us is greater than our divisions, and that our language always seeks to point to truths beyond our words. Amen.

Let us give thanks today for the most precious gift of all — life. May we remember that this planet has been loaned to us; we do not own it. We are grateful for its beauty. Teach us to be good stewards of our earth. Amen.

We are grateful for the gifts of love in our lives — families and friends, animals and plants, communities of diverse values and beliefs. Teach us to honour our diversities yet always seek common ground. Amen.

Help us, Creator Spirit, to be grateful for sunlight and flowers, streams and rivers and oceans; the moon and planets, this and all countless galaxies. We thank You for the great silent Light from which all began. Teach us to be humble. Now, in silence, we come with abundant thanks [*Silence . . .*] Amen.

PRAYERS FOR MEALTIME

It is important to gather together for a shared meal as a family or small group, once a day if that is possible.

Before beginning to eat, ask the family to spend a few moments of silence together. Then, light a candle and ask anyone who wishes to say a few words expressing their thanks, concerns, or sorrows. When everyone has had a chance, close with some of these words:

O God, giver of life, we thank You for this gathering and for all whom we love who are not with us today. We thank You for this food and for those who harvested and prepared it. We ask that we may go from this place with a renewed sense of Your presence in our midst, as individuals and as a people gathered together in Your name. Amen.

O God, we recall that we are one in Your eyes and we celebrate this unity in our common meal. Our many blessings cause us to give You thanks. May Your gifts strengthen us in our task of serving You and the world. Amen.

Spirit of the Living God, let us bless and keep one another as if tomorrow might never come. Let us be generous to one another as if nothing mattered but love. Let us walk together remembering the life and teachings of Jesus. Amen.

Eternal and loving God, we give thanks for being; we give thanks for being here; we give thanks for being here together. Amen.

PRAYERS FOR AND WITH CHILDREN

Mealtime Prayers

God, we thank You for food, family and friends. Amen.

For this food, God, we give thanks. We also thank You for (*name*). Amen.

Bless us, O God, as we eat. And bless all the children of the world. Amen.

Bedtime Prayers

For the moon and stars and evening light;
For day gone by and calming night;
For family, friends, and creatures, too,
We rest our hearts in You. Amen.

Now night has come and I must sleep,
I pray You know my soul to keep,
And when the morning light appears,
I wake to find You still are near. Amen.

Day is done, night has come.
Stars are here, sleep is near.
Keep me safely in Thy care,
'Til morning light so fair. Amen.

A Prayer for Animals

O God, take care of my animal friends.
Guard and keep them safe from all harm.
Be with those who are sick or lonely or
without homes. And let me be their friend. Amen

POSTLUDE

It is our hope that this book will have been of help as you develop your own personal prayer life and also inspire you to become part of a small group. Our desire was to deepen your commitment to the life and teachings of Jesus and to encourage you to explore discipleship further.

We realize that prayer is a lifetime discipline, so while this beginning is very important, it is only one step among many others. To continue your prayer life, you could go back to Day One and start again (there is nothing wrong with repetition), but as you pray the prayers here, do please add your own. We suggest beginning with Day One with your own words and continuing through to Day Thirty-One. It may be that over time you will not need this prayer-book, nor any other . . .

CONCLUDING PRAYER

The LORD is on my side; I will not fear...I shall not die, but live.

Psalm 118:6, 17 (KJV)

Be of good cheer. It is I; be not afraid.

Mark 6:50 (KJV)

Peace I leave you, my peace I give unto you; not as the world giveth...Let not your heart be troubled, neither let it be afraid...Arise, let us go hence.

John 14:27, 31 (KJV)

O God, stay with all those who seek to follow You, who stand for life and love and justice. Be present with those who call on You, as well as those who do not know Your name. Let the hearts of those who seek You find comfort and courage for daily living, and for the abundant life to come. Amen.

Be of good cheer. Do not be afraid. For He is in our midst even now! Amen.

APPENDIX
AN EVENTIDE SERVICE

AN EVENTIDE SERVICE

This service was written in May 2005 by John and Richard Morgan near Tintern Abbey, Wales, but it was inspired by an eventide service at Westminster Abbey, London, England. Although it was written with people eligible for concessionary prices and entrance fees in mind, i.e. those who, for whatever reason, are on very low incomes, it can be adapted to focus on different themes.

¶ *Call to Worship (with bell and the lighting of a candle):*

O God, we gather knowing in our hearts how far short we have fallen from what You desire for us — to love You and each other and ourselves. Cleanse our hearts of all dark secrets and bring to light those acts whose consequences have injured others. Tame our strong wills with the soft presence of Your forgiveness, so that we may face You and each other with souls made whole by Your grace. Now in quiet reflection, we direct our attention to Your presence in our midst.

Service Leader: Lord, keep us always mindful of Your presence, even when we have strayed.

People: Lord, have mercy upon us.

Service Leader: Lord, let us know that only one thing is required of us: To love You and each other.

People: Lord, keep us mindful of Your law, written on our hearts.

Service Leader: Lord, let us remember that no one enters Your kingdom by walking past their neighbour, especially those who are old, disabled, unemployed, or without the means to support themselves.

People: Lord, keep our eyes upon You and all Your creation, that we may be innkeepers in Your Holy House.

Service Leader: The Lord be with you.

People: And with you and all we love, in this life and the next.

All: Amen.

¶ *Here a hymn may be sung or a piece of music played.*

¶ *Readings: Psalm 71:1–4; 9–13; 18. Psalm 90.*

¶ *Silence*

¶ *Readings: Mark 12:29–31; Luke 18:1–6*

¶ *Silence*

¶ *Here may follow prayers for healing and restoration.*

Service Leader: O Lord, we come before You broken in mind, body, or spirit, but yearning for Your healing touch.

People: Instil in us, God, a contrite heart, knowing that what You have given us to bear may break our hearts, but also that You will not leave us without hope.

Service Leader: The Lord refresh and heal your spirit.

¶ *Readings: Matthew 5:1–12*

¶ *Silence*

Service Leader: Compassionate God, You never turn away from anyone in need and always have love for those society disregards. We confess that we have often walked past others, rather than stopped to help them. We have worshipped power, status, and our own desires first, forgetting that Your kingdom blesses the poor in spirit, those who mourn, the meek and merciful, the pure in heart, the peacemakers, and those who cry out for justice.

Service Leader: Lord have mercy upon us.

People: Christ have mercy upon us and grant us courage.

Service Leader: Make it so, Lord, for all people.

All: Amen.

¶ *Here a hymn may be sung or a piece of music played.*

Service Leader: May the Lord grant you the courage to act for justice, the heart to feel the sufferings of others, and the strength to act.

People: Lord, grant us courage.

Service Leader: Now go to honour God and your soul by serving others in word and deed, so that all creation may be made whole.

People: Grant us peace.

Service Leader: Go with courage and peace to serve others, remembering that the spirit of Christ is in every creature and all the universe.

¶ *Sound the bell and extinguish the candle. People leave in silence, one by one, in single file.*